D1067740

MICKEY
MANTLE

other titles in the **BIOGRAPHY**® *book series:*

Muhammad Ali

Al Capone

Katharine Hepburn

Martin Luther King, Jr.

Jacqueline Kennedy Onassis

Pope John Paul II

Ronald Reagan

MICKEY MANTLE

Phil Berger

A Balliett & Fitzgerald Book

PARK LANE

NEW YORK

Copyright © 1998 by Random House Value Publishing, Inc.
All rights reserved under International and Pan-American Copyright Conventions.

No part of this book may be reproduced or transmitted in any form or by any means,
electronic or mechanical, including photocopying, recording, or by any information
storage and retrieval system, without permission in writing from the publisher.

This 1998 edition is published by Park Lane Press,
a division of Random House Value Publishing, Inc.,
a Random House Company
201 East 50th Street, New York, New York 10022

A&E's acclaimed BIOGRAPHY series is available on videocassette from
A&E Home Video. Call 1-800-423-1212 to order.

A&E and **BIOGRAPHY** are trademarks of A&E Television Networks,
registered in the United States and other countries.

Park Lane Press and colophon are trademarks of
Random House Value Publishing, Inc.

Random House, Inc.
New York • Toronto • London • Sydney • Auckland
www.randomhouse.com

Printed and bound in the United States of America

A Balliett & Fitzgerald Book
Series Editor: Thomas Dyja
Book Design: Lisa Govan, Susan Canavan
Production Editors: Maria Fernandez, Mike Walters
Photo Research: Maria Fernandez
Assistant Editor: Irene Agriodimas

Library of Congress Cataloging-in-Publication Data

Berger, Phil.
    Mickey Mantle / Phil Berger.   —1st ed.
            p.   cm.   —(Biography)
    "A Balliett & Fitzgerald book."
        Includes bibliographical (p. 168) references and index.
    1. Mantle, Mickey, 1931–1995. 2. Baseball players—
United States—Biography. 3. New York Yankees (baseball team)
I. Title. II. Series: Biography (Park Lane Press)
GV865.M33B47   1998
796.357.092—dc21
    (B)   96-20175
                                                                CIP

ISBN 0-517-20099-6
10 9 8 7 6 5 4 3 2 1
First Edition

CONTENTS

At home in Commerce, Oklahoma

CHAPTER ONE

HUMBLE BEGINNINGS

---◆---

Mickey Mantle was born in the midst of the Great Depression, on October 20, 1931. His birthplace—Spavinaw, Oklahoma, population 213—was one of a number of small mining towns in the northeastern corner of Oklahoma where the state converges with Missouri and Kansas and Dust Bowl Okies not unlike those in John Steinbeck's *The Grapes of Wrath* eked out a living.

For most folks, including Mantle's father, Elvin Clark Mantle, that eventually meant going down into the zinc and lead mines of the Eagle-Picher company. The company's mines were linked by underground tunnels that ran through those Okie towns all the way to Joplin, Missouri. Mining was a hard day's work—eight hours in congested chambers deep underground, for money that amounted to bare-bones-survival wages, as little as $30 a week. Miners toiled in mortal fear of cave-ins.

The long-term peril was just as unsettling—breathing the dank air shot through with minute zinc and lead particles was ruinous to a man's health. Many a miner fell victim to cancer or tuberculosis well before his hair turned gray.

Men like Mantle's father, who was known as "Mutt," took a fatalistic attitude about their hard lives: Live while you can, and damn the consequences. They didn't gripe, or beat their breasts. They carried on as best they could and often with a perverse need, it seemed, to challenge the grim facts of their daily labors. How else to account for the fact that so many of them, Mutt included, chain-smoked cigarettes when common sense said tobacco could only exacerbate peril to lungs that were already in jeopardy?

The Mantles—Mutt; his wife, Lovell; and their first child, little Mickey—would move forty-five miles northeast to Commerce, population 2,242, when the boy was four. They settled into a two-bedroom clapboard house with a small front porch and garage at 319 North Quincy Street, hard by the pebbly refuse mounds, known as "chat" piles, common to that lead-and-zinc-mining country. Like their house in Spavinaw, this one had no indoor plumbing.

Mutt worked as a shoveler in a mine called Blue Goose Number One. He was a quiet, principled man who refused to buy groceries on credit, preferring to cash his check and pay hard dollars. Mickey was ever aware of his father's struggle to provide for the Mantle brood, who, besides himself, came to include twin brothers Roy and Ray; youngest brother Larry (known as Butch); and a sister, Barbara. Mickey's siblings were four to nine years younger than he. Mutt's dad, Charlie, who had been a butcher by trade, also stayed at the house in Commerce, and sometimes a half brother, Theodore—the product of Lovell's failed first marriage—stopped by.

Although he would prove to be Mutt's favorite, Mickey was always close to his siblings. The Mantle kids, Barbara included, would divide up and play football and other sports or, goaded by Mickey, put on makeshift boxing gloves made from multiple pairs of socks and fight one another.

For all the fun they had, the Mantle children were aware of the daily struggle for the family's bread.

"Kids nowadays don't have any idea of what the Depression was like—it's just a word in the history books—and that's great," said Mantle. "But it was a hard time to bring up a family, especially where we lived, which was one of the poorest parts of the country. Even in wealthy parts of the country, people were standing on line for food. Finding work and earning money was the hardest thing in the world to do, and keeping a family alive and fed and happy at the same time was even harder. But he did both, he and my mother. . . . She was pretty brave, too; she had to make do without very much—she did all our cooking on a wood stove, for one thing—but we never felt we were without anything. He never quit, never admitted defeat."

Mickey could not help but admire his father for his refusal to be daunted by this hard life.

"No boy, I think, ever loved his father more than I did," said Mantle. "I was a good boy, really, who needed little disciplining, and I would do nearly anything to keep my father happy. He was a big, strong, stern-looking man, just a fraction short of 6 feet tall, lean and well muscled, with the strong, gnarled hands of a miner, and dark, thick hair. . . . He never had to raise his hand to me to make me obey, for I needed only a sharp look and a word from him and the knowledge that I had displeased him to make me go and do better."

Mutt Mantle had one abiding passion, and that was baseball. He pored through the box scores in the sports pages of the *Daily*

Oklahoman, the only section of the newspaper that really interested him. As Mickey would recall: "Baseball, that's all he lived for. He used to say that it seemed to him like he just died in the winter, until the time when baseball came around again."

The miners—Blue Goose, West Side, and the other Eagle-Picher shafts—fielded baseball teams that regularly competed against one another. Games took place on Wednesday evenings or Sunday afternoons, with a keg of beer to the winners. Mutt, who could play every position, usually pitched for the Blue Goose team. His brother Eugene, known as Tunney, was his catcher.

Mutt's passion for the game ran so deep that early on he made a conscious decision to train Mickey to be a major-league baseball player. Indeed, the boy was named after Mutt's favorite ballplayer, Mickey Cochrane, the hard-hitting catcher of the Philadelphia Athletics, whose real name was Gordon Stanley Cochrane.

Mantle's mother, Lovell, shared her husband's pleasure in the game, often doing her household chores while listening to broadcasts of the St. Louis Cardinal games and then recounting them to the family at dinnertime. While Mickey was still an infant, at Mutt's request Lovell fashioned a baseball cap out of cotton cloth. "It wasn't much to look at and a sight to see after Mickey chewed it up, but, so far as his father was concerned, the child was a big-leaguer every time he wore it," she said.

When Mickey was three, Mutt asked his wife to make Mickey's first baseball uniform. With money scarce, Mutt sacrificed the pants of his own baseball uniform so his son would look like a ballplayer.

"Dad insisted on my being taught the positions on a baseball field before the ABC's," Mantle said. "He was that crazy about baseball. . . . I was probably the only baby in history whose first lullaby was the radio broadcast of a ball game. One night, Mama says, I woke up during the seventh-inning stretch. She pleaded with Dad to please cut off that contraption and let me sleep.

"'You got Mickey wrong, hon,' Dad said. 'I don't blame him for screaming. He knew the situation called for a bunt instead of hitting away.'"

By the time Mickey was in first grade, his baseball education had begun in earnest. Mutt would get home from Blue Goose Number One at four o'clock in the afternoon, and Mickey would hurry out into the front yard. Mutt had already bought his son a miniature bat and, in deference to the boy's delicate age, would challenge his hitting ability with tennis balls. For hours, Mutt, a right-handed pitcher, and Mickey's grandfather, Charlie, a left-hander, would pitch to Mickey, scoring his hits according to the idiosyncracies of their North Quincy Street setting.

Mickey (right) and Mutt together on the front porch.

"A ground ball, pop, and strikeout were outs," recalled Mantle. "A line drive off the side of the house, a double; off the roof, a triple; and into the trees [in the adjoining lot], a homer."

Although Mutt was not given to expressing love, Mickey nonetheless believed in his father's deep feelings for him. Early on he saw Mutt's intense—even obsessive—efforts to make him a baseball player as being for his own good, and his own responses as being a way to hold a father's love. Through baseball, Mutt believed, and his son came to understand, Mickey Charles might have a chance to escape a miner's hard existence.

But while Mantle appreciated what Mutt's objectives were, and worked hard to satisfy them, there were subtle psychological forces at play. Baseball was fun, and would remain fun, Mickey insisted, but at the same time he never could relent in the quest to perfect his skills. And that unrelenting need to excel, the better to please his father, would generate a pressure that would leave a mark on the boy, and later on the man Mickey Mantle became.

❧ ❧ ❧

"... I wanted to please him."

Day after day, Mutt and Grandpa Charlie kept working on Mickey's hitting and other facets of his game, and often it wouldn't be until 9:00 P.M. that they would break for supper. Lovell would do her share by making the small, skinny boy his uniforms out of old clothes and his baseball shoes by screwing in makeshift cleats. Mutt kept the growing Mickey supplied with a hitter's tools by taking bats broken in his miners' games and cutting them down to size, and at Christmas would buy the boy a new baseball glove. Later, Roy and Ray became involved, too, shagging after the line drives and towering flies that Mickey walloped off the serves of Mutt and Grandpa Charlie, both of whom threw with some velocity. No pitty-pat pitches for young Mick.

The hard work made a baseball prodigy of Mickey. As a grade-schooler he excelled in a local Pee Wee League. When he was eleven years old he was regarded as so unique a talent that the age minimum of twelve was waived so Mickey could play for the Ottawa County Commerce-Picher team of the Gabby Street League, named after the former major-league catcher and manager Charles Evard Street. By then young Mantle was an accomplished switch-hitter.

If he wasn't playing in organized leagues, Mantle would work up improvised two- or three-man games resembling baseball—Pitch and Catch, Annie Over, and Major League—in which he and his friends used broom handles and tennis balls and Mickey pretended to be each player in the Boston Red Sox batting order—Jimmy Foxx, Bobby Doerr, Joe Cronin, Dom DiMaggio, and, of course, the great Ted Williams. His preference for the Red Sox was based on his devotion to that pure hitter, Williams, who in 1941 would bat .406—the last major leaguer to hit .400.

During the early forties, Mickey and pals Nick Ferguson and LeRoy Bennett played for a Gabby Street League team in Douthat, hiking the three miles to get to the ballpark. They would have gladly traversed twice the distance if they had to. As Mantle recalled: "The kids ranged in ages from twelve to eighteen. Strictly amateur, although you'd never know from the size of the crowds. A whole mob used to drive out, mostly min-ing people and their families.

One year, Mantle's team won the league title and got to meet

THE EDUCATION OF A SWITCH-HITTER

Mutt Mantle was determined to make his son Mickey into a hitter who was as fluid from the left side of home plate as from the right side.

When the right handed Mutt pitched, Mickey batted lefty. Against his southpaw grandfather, a onetime sandlot player, he batted right handed, his natural preference.

For a while, Mickey was resistant to changing from his right handed stance, even if Mutt felt it would give him a better "look" at curveballs. By that, Mutt was referring to the way a curveball breaks as it speeds toward a batter. That abrupt "break" could be daunting to a hitter—and certainly was a challenge—as Roger Kahn would explain in *Esquire* magazine:

"When a right-handed batter faces a right handed pitcher, the ball seems to be coming toward his ear. Then, as the batter fights a reflex to duck, the curve breaks down and across the plate. The batter sets himself and digs his heel spikes into the ground. Now the pitcher throws a fastball at the chin. In this frightening game, the pitcher holds the wild cards. But when a left-handed batter stands in against a right-hander,

the balance turns. The ball seems to be coming from the outside. "You see it real good out there," hitters say. A curve breaking inward can be a fine pitch, but the illusion of impending concussion is lost. Everybody hits better from the opposite side."

Mutt may also have had a prophetic flash of baseball's future, envisioning a time when managers would platoon players according to whether a righthander or a left-hander was pitching. To be a switch-hitter would override this tactical obstacle to playing every day.

Whatever Mutt's reasons were for making Mickey a switch-hitter, the boy continued to resist, finding it awkward to try swinging from the left side of the plate.

"In Dad's book there was only one way I could be 'bad,'" recalled Mantle. "That's when I batted right handed against a righthanded pitcher. I did it once when I was ten years old, when Dad was in the stands. 'Go on home,' he hollered at me, 'and don't you ever put on that baseball uniform again until you switch-hit like I taught you.'"

Gabby Street himself at the awards banquet at the end of the season. Street had played from 1904 to 1912 for Cincinnati and Boston in the National League and for Washington and New York in the American League, and later managed the Cardinals and the Browns.

For Mantle this was the first major leaguer he had ever met, and Street didn't disappoint. He told them about life in the "bigs" as well as a story of the time in the 1920s when he agreed to attempt to catch a baseball with his bare hands as it was dropped from the top of the Empire State Building. In ten tries, Street said, he had managed to hang on to just one.

It was not the young Mantle's only brush with major-league baseball. Every so often, when Mutt had put aside the money for it, he would drive up to St. Louis for the weekend in the family's beat-up 1935 LaSalle so Mickey and he could catch the Cardinals on a Saturday night and then again for a Sunday doubleheader. "To me," said Mantle, "this was like a journey to the Big Rock Candy Mountain. It meant an early bath on Saturday, then getting into a clean T-shirt, clean blue jeans, and my beloved baseball cap."

That cap, with its bill creased, topped Mantle's blond head nearly every waking hour and marked him for the baseball diehard he was. Mickey pursued his dream in a small-town setting that hadn't much to divert him from it. Commerce's main drag ran but a few blocks and consisted of a handful of stores, City Hall, the Black Cat café, a movie theater, and a pool hall where Mickey would hang out with his friends. There were weekend dances for the young folks—music by jukebox—but Mickey was painfully shy and reluctant to try the latest steps. On Sundays there were Bible study classes and prayer meetings.

While in later years Mickey tended to portray his childhood as idyllic, there were some who saw it not quite as picture-book perfect as Mantle made out. His wife, Merlyn, would observe: "And yet the early pressure on Mickey to play ball, and his self-imposed drive to play it better than anyone, caused real emotional problems for him. A lot of the conflicts in him later had their roots in those years. Mick wet his bed until he was sixteen years old.

"I would hope that this would not be taken as demeaning him. But it is important, I think, in understanding what he went through, and how much he wanted to please his dad. This is what the pressure of wanting that approval did to him. He told me that he knew from the time he was five years old that he wanted to be a ballplayer, and how he could never face his father if he didn't make it to the major leagues."

In 1944, the innocence of Mantle's boyhood was jolted when Grandpa Charlie died of Hodgkin's disease, a form of cancer that affects the lymph nodes and eventually attacks the bone marrow. Mantle saw his once-vigorous grandfather decline before his eyes. The family's susceptibility to Hodgkin's became even more obvious to Mantle when his Uncle Tunney died of it a few years later.

By '44 Mutt had swapped the family's house in town for a farm on the outskirts of Commerce. The 160 acres belonged to another man, and Mutt, acting as a sharecropper, hoped to make a living off the land to escape a miner's life.

"It wasn't much of a farm—we lived in Dust Bowl country and a lot of people had quit and gone to California," said Mantle. "But he thought maybe a farm might mean a better life for us kids." Mutt planted wheat, oats, corn; Mickey and his brothers would milk the cows and bring the buckets to their mother, who would separate the milk from the cream. As their first harvest approached, the Mantles were in high spirits.

But as Mantle recalled: "The very first year, there was a

flood and the river came up over the farm and ruined it. My father just picked up, went back into town and down into the mines again." The family would move to a little shack in Whitebird, a tiny village near Commerce. It took four trips with a horse-drawn wagon to complete the move, and Mickey would never forget the grim expression on his father's face at this painful turn in the family's fortunes.

❦ ❦ ❦

"The hell you are."

The primitive dwelling in Whitebird had no indoor plumbing, and a small kitchen would be added on later. Yet difficult as life could be during the Oklahoma winters, with the winds whipping across the plains and only a wood-burning stove to warm them, or in the blazing hot summers when flies swarmed their living space, the Mantles carried on.

As Mickey said, "We never realized that we were missing anything. And I don't guess we did miss anything that was too important. We didn't have TV and transistors and sports cars and new clothes. But we had food to eat, we liked each other, and we had fun."

Mickey enrolled at Commerce High School and quickly made a name for himself as an all-around athlete, playing basketball, football, and baseball. As a basketball player, "Little Mickey"—he was several inches shy of his adult height of 5 feet, 11½ inches—was the ball-handling, penetrating guard of the fast-breaking quintet—a true point guard before the term was coined.

As a halfback, Mantle's speed and sure hands made him a natural at that position in Coach Alan Woolard's T-formation offense, which in an era of single-wing attacks was considered new-fangled.

Mutt was not enamored of his son playing football, fearing an injury could derail Mickey from that big-league baseball career for which he had spent years preparing his son. But he could not bring himself to forbid Mickey from donning the pads and helmet for the Commerce eleven.

On game days—whatever the sport—Mutt and Lovell would be in the stands rooting their son on. "My folks were always involved," Mantle said. "They loved every minute of it. And Mom used to rant and rave at those games. . . . If she objected to a referee's decision, you could hear her voice travel across the gym: 'Where are your glasses, you bum?' Believe me, if the referee called anything against Commerce, she'd cuss him out like a sailor. It unnerved my father. He'd cover his head with his hands and sit a few rows behind her to get away from the shouting."

Later on, when the twins, Roy and Ray, were playing football for Commerce High and a game against Afton High ended in an altercation that had Roy in the midst of it, Lovell ran down to the field and swung her pocketbook against the helmets of the Afton boys bent on doing harm to her little boy.

While he was a freshman at Commerce, Mantle sustained an injury that almost made Mutt's forebodings prophetic. In a scrimmage, a tackler kicked him in the left leg as he carried the ball. Mantle was helped off the field. Later at home, he soaked his swollen ankle in buckets of hot water. But the swelling increased and overnight he developed a temperature of 104 degrees. Alarmed, Mutt drove him to the hospital in Picher, where Mickey was confined for two weeks while various treatments failed to reduce the swelling.

Each day Lovell would walk a mile from Whitebird to catch

Roy and Ray Mantle, with their baseball-playing brother.

a bus that would get her to the hospital. When Mutt arrived after work to be at Mickey's bedside, she would head back to Whitebird to attend to the other Mantle children.

After two weeks the doctors had not solved Mickey's problem, but they had a name for it. Osteomyelitis—a staph infection of the bone marrow. When they hinted to Lovell that the only solution for the badly abscessed bone might be to amputate the leg, she told them, "The hell you are."

By that afternoon, Mutt had checked Mickey out of the Picher hospital and bundled him up in the LaSalle for the long drive to the Crippled Children's Hospital in Oklahoma City, a hospital for patients who couldn't afford to pay.

For Mickey, the injury brought fear and depression. But it was at the Oklahoma City hospital that doctors tried the wonder drug penicillin and got results. The swelling abated and, though Mantle would lose twenty pounds—he left the hospital weighing 110 pounds—he was on the slow road to recovery.

❖ ❖ ❖

"*I believe I can make him what you want him to be.*"

To get around at first, Mantle needed crutches. But in time he was once again playing baseball, now with even greater fervor, as though that broad hint of his own mortality had left him determined to pursue the game—and the dream it encapsulated—unrelentingly.

As Mantle recalled: "I drove myself to get better and better, regardless of time and circumstance. I had to swing that bat and field my position better than any kid around. So that's all I did: play, play, play. I had no other enjoyment. Nothing was more important."

This put him in synch with Mutt, who continued to work him hard in practices and then would watch Mickey as he pitched and played shortstop for the Commerce High varsity and, by the summer of 1947, played second base for the Miami (Oklahoma) squad in the Ban Johnson League for players twenty-one years old and under. The Ban Johnson League, named after the early American League president, recruited college players and top amateurs from the tristate area (Oklahoma, Kansas, Missouri) and had been set up by a miner from Baxter Springs, Kansas, named Barney Barnett.

Like Mutt, Barnett was devoted to baseball. As a player, he had made it only as far as Burlington of the Three-I League, but as coach of the Baxter Springs Whiz Kids—regarded as the top team in the league—he took delight in cultivating young talent. When he saw Mantle play for the Miami team, he was impressed enough to ask him to join the Whiz Kids. And then he reinforced his recruiting pitch by taking Mutt aside.

As Barnett would recall: "I told him, 'Mutt, you got to give Mickey to me. I believe I can make him what you want him to be.' I still remember Mickey's father sticking out his chest and busting out in a big laugh. 'He's all yours, Barney. You're the man who can bring in the big-league scouts.'"

In fact, major-league scouts did look over the Ban Johnson talent when they happened to pass through Baxter Springs. Barney and his league drew that kind of recognition from organized baseball. So when Barnett had approached Mickey—now a mature 160 pounds—to be a Whiz Kid, it was an important first step on the yellow brick road to the big time.

The Whiz Kids played not only in the Ban Johnson League but in outside games as well, a busy schedule that took them north into Missouri and as far south as Bentonville, Arkansas. Sometimes they lined up against the various miners teams from the area.

The field at Baxter Springs had a natural boundary, the Spring River. Where the river flowed in center field it was a good 400 feet from home plate; in right field it ran to 500 feet. One Sunday afternoon in 1948, with the river threatening to overrun its banks, Mantle hit three home runs that landed in the water, two batting from the left-hand side of the plate, the other from the right-hand side. The feat left the roughly 200 spectators so amazed that one of them thought it appropriate to pass a hat through the grandstand to let the fans show their appreciation. Fifty-four dollars was the amount Mickey pocketed that day—more money, he was to say, than he had ever seen before at one time.

It seemed an innocent enough gesture. But Mantle's windfall would have reverberations in Oklahoma City once the state athletic commission there learned about it. Mickey was declared to have forfeited his amateur status by accepting the money, and only through the heartfelt arguments of Mutt did the commission reverse its ruling and restore Mickey's eligibility. The commission stipulated that Mantle had to return the money. Whether he did is moot. Suffice it to say that there are those who insist that the return of the $54 was done in a way that "looked good on paper."

Whatever.

By now Mantle had begun to draw the attention of those scouts passing through Baxter Springs. One of them was Tom Greenwade, a gaunt man given to wearing a white shirt and tie while covering Missouri, Oklahoma, Kansas, and Arkansas for the New York Yankees. As a poor boy growing up in Kansas, Greenwade had discovered his throwing arm by hunting rabbits with rocks he unleashed at startling speed. That knack was, he found, adaptable to the baseball diamond. Greenwade had been a minor-league pitcher until a bout of typhoid nearly did him in. Neither law school nor a stint with the IRS during the gangster era satisfied him. But cruising through the Midwest in his late-model Cadillac, looking to scare up talent for the big leagues—well, that was more to his liking.

He was first hired by the St. Louis Browns, then by the Brooklyn Dodgers, whose general manager, Branch Rickey, had him combing the Negro Leagues in search of a player to break the color line. Yes, Greenwade had scouted Jackie Robinson and, as his son Bunch would say, "Dad decided Jackie Robinson had more heart and more physical ability than any other player."

In '48, as Robinson was switched to second base, Tom Greenwade was in Baxter Springs scouting the Whiz Kids.

"I went over to see him play at Alba, Missouri, but I wasn't particularly impressed," recalled Greenwade. "The boy was only sixteen then and hadn't his full growth."

Mantle's version of when Greenwade made his first appearance differed. He put Greenwade in Baxter Springs on a day in 1948 on which The Mick hit two home runs into the river. Later, as rain fell and Mantle ducked into the family car to avoid getting wet, Mutt knocked at the window and said a fella wanted to meet him. That was Greenwade, according to Mickey, and the Yankee scout told him that because Mantle was still in high school, he couldn't make him an offer. But, as Mantle told it, Greenwade said not to sign with any other team—come Mickey's graduation day, Tom Greenwade would be back. Mutt wondered if he would make an offer at that time. Greenwade gave a noncommittal answer.

It left the Mantles wondering whether Greenwade's interest was genuine. Mutt wasn't sure, but he liked the idea of Mickey's being part of the long and storied Yankee tradition.

❧ ❧ ❧

"... a classic illustration of the American Dream"

Senior year, 1949, at Commerce wound down. Mickey played varsity football, basketball, and baseball. He gave perfunctory attention to his studies, but his baseball progress was going strong. In the spring of that year, Yankee scout Greenwade reappeared in Commerce to pick up Mantle's trail. By then Mickey, who was playing shortstop, had grown. He had a man's strength in those broad shoulders and thick forearms that enabled him to drive a baseball an Oklahoma country mile.

Later that month, on the night Mickey was due to graduate, Greenwade was back, hoping to see Mickey play with the Whiz Kids in Coffeyville, Kansas, the hometown of Hall of Fame pitcher Walter (Big Train) Johnson. Mutt arranged for his son to be excused from the graduation exercises so Greenwade could take another look that, with any luck, might lead to an offer on behalf of the Yankee organization.

Greenwade took a couple of looks that Friday night in Coffeyville, and again on Sunday in Baxter Springs. It was in Baxter Springs that Greenwade saw Mantle bat right-handed for the first time, and it was only then that he realized the boy was a switch-hitter, as powerful from one side of the plate as the other, for in Baxter Springs, Mantle hit four powerful drives that cinched the deal, so to speak.

Immediately after the game, Mutt and Greenwade sat down in the scout's Cadillac, parked behind the grandstand, and haggled over the financial details of Mickey's signing with the Yankee organization. Greenwade offered $400 for the remainder of the season. Mutt argued that Mantle could make more working in the mines and playing semipro baseball on weekends. The scout offered to sweeten the deal.

"I disremember what the exact amount was," said Greenwade. "But I know we figured out what Mickey's salary would be for the remainder of the season with Independence [of the Kansas-Oklahoma-Missouri League], and it came to around $400. To avoid the bonus rule then in effect, a boy signed to a Class D contract couldn't receive more than $1,500 for bonus and salary in his first year, and we were mighty careful to keep it under that. A dollar or two more would have put him in the bonus class."

In those days, baseball teams often paid substantial bonuses to untried prospects. Not long after Mantle signed with New York, Paul Pettit became one of the most publicized of the "bonus babies," as they were called, when the Pittsburgh Pirates signed him for a bonus reported to be $90,000 to $100,000. But the rules back then required a bonus baby to be placed immediately on the roster of the major-league team that signed him and stay with that parent team for two years. Usually such players were a long way from being ready for major-league competition, so the two years became dead time, with the bonus baby pining away on the bench. In effect, the rule kept the bonus baby from developing his skills in minor leagues that would have been more suited to his experience and skill level. So the fat bonus was a double-edged sword. The instant gratification of substantial money might prove ruinous to a prospect's development. For every future star such as

Mickey's mother, Lovell, pours him a glass of milk.

Harmon Killebrew or Jackie Jensen who took the money and eventually found stardom in the major leagues, there were plenty of others, such as Pettit, and Frank Leja and Tommy Carroll with the Yankees, who were flops.

But Mantle was not saddled by such restrictions. As a young prospect he was free to develop in the Yankees' minor-league chain according to his talent. In the best of circumstances the experience would provide the testing by which, with each passing season, he would develop as a ballplayer, "stretching" his talent until the top brass would see the wisdom of moving him to the Yankee team itself.

On the night he signed him, Greenwade, who was a shrewd negotiator and tight with his and the Yankees' money, expressed to Mutt certain doubts about his son's potential. He did so to make a deal at a price that would serve the Yankee organization, for as Greenwade later admitted: "I don't quite know how to put it, but what I'm trying to tell you is that I know now how [Yankee scout] Paul Krichell felt when he first saw Lou Gehrig. Paul told me once that the first time he saw Gehrig he knew that as a scout he'd never have another moment like it. I felt the same about Mantle."

Indeed, years later with Mantle a Yankee legend, Greenwade's signing of this country boy would take on a golden glow. In the words of David Halberstam, it was "a classic scene, straight out of Norman Rockwell. . . . The myth of Tom Greenwade, the greatest scout of his age, blended with Mantle's myth to create a classic illustration of the American Dream: For every American of talent, no matter how poor or simple his or her background, there is always a Tom Greenwade out there searching to discover that person and help him or her find a rightful place among the stars."

At the time, though—back in 1949—Mantle's future was

hardly guaranteed. While any scout could see he had raw power and speed, Mantle's play at shortstop was erratic. And it was far too soon to predict whether that power of his would translate against pitching that was bound, on each succeeding level, to be superior to that which Mantle had hit so easily in the Ban Johnson League. The road to the major leagues was littered with men who returned to their hometowns for some failing serious enough to remove them from major-league consideration.

At the outset, Mantle would test himself at the lowest level of the baseball feeding chain, in Class D. When Greenwade had zeroed in on exactly where Mantle would start out, he'd mentioned to Mutt the Yankees' Class D teams in Macallister, Oklahoma, and in Independence, Kansas. Since Independence was closer—only 170 miles from Commerce—Mutt said he wanted his boy at Independence.

On a day soon after Mickey's signing with the Yankees' organization, Mutt made the drive with him to Independence. He walked him up to the room of the team's manager, Harry Craft, in the Darby Hotel. The manager shook hands with both Mantles. Then Mutt told Mickey: "From now on, Mr. Craft is your boss. I want you to do just as he tells you and pay attention to what he says, just as if I were saying it myself. And I want you to play this game just the way you would play it if I were here to watch you."

Mickey Mantle was alone and on his own. His baseball career was about to begin.

For many of those who loved their baseball but didn't live within range of a big-league ballpark, the minor leagues were as near as they could get to the real thing. Most of them got their flavor of big-league baseball from radio broadcasts, which left a lot to the imagination of the listener. If you wanted a more direct association with the trim green grass of the infield, the echoing crack of bat against ball, the savory scent of hot dogs, the roar of the crowd—well, a minor-league game provided all those and more.

For Americans back then, a minor-league team was an extension of the community, an entity in which the locals could take civic pride. This country was smaller in '49, its people more cloistered than they would be in the coming decades. The popularity of air travel, the accessibility to superhighways for cars, the expansion of media coverage—in time all those developments would make a larger world shrink and become readily accessible to mainstream America. The minor leagues paid the price for that change.

Television, of course, figured prominently in the decline of the minor leagues. From the late forties on, TV's expanded coverage of the major leagues left less and less of baseball to the imagination. Why go see the local minor-league players when, with the flick of a dial, there was Ted Williams, Joe DiMaggio, Jackie Robinson right there in your living room?

The other factor that put a dent in the popularity of the minor leagues was the rampant spending by major-league teams on untried talent—those "bonus babies." To curb their indiscriminate spending through bidding wars for inexperienced players and to get a grip on their economies, baseball owners made certain changes.

In 1962 the major leagues adopted a player development plan requiring each big-league team to have five farm teams. That number was supposed to guarantee at least 100 minor-league teams—at a time when the minor leagues were becoming an endangered species. By 1963 the minor leagues were no longer a local attraction, supported by a small town's hunger for baseball and its civic pride. The minor leagues had become a training ground for future major leaguers—a very cut-and-dried proposition. From 461 minor-league teams in 1949, when Mantle was at Independence, by 1963 the number had gone down to only 127 teams. And in 1965, with the advent of a player draft by which major-league teams now could draft the negotiation rights to high school and college players, the new bean-counting approach was reinforced.

But in 1949, all those developments lay ahead. When Mickey Mantle turned up at Independence, a minor-league baseball player still had an allure to the populace that was disproportionate to the measly wages he was earning. To the folks of whatever hamlet his team represented, he was a hero.

circa 1950

CHAPTER TWO

IN THE MINORS

O n his arrival in Kansas, Mantle felt less like a hero and more like a shy and lonely country boy, a bit shaken at being away from his familiar home turf, removed from the reassuring presence of his parents. But once he met his teammates, the affable Mickey—quiet and unassuming though he was— became comfortable enough with his new team. Why not? He was doing exactly what he'd been trained to do since he was a first-grader at Central Grade School in Commerce. Mantle started slowly at Independence, but soon enough had his batting average up around the .300 mark, flashing occasional power. But as capably as he was performing in the K-O-M League, Mantle was not without his problems. As manager Craft would recall: "Mickey . . . had plenty to learn even though he learned fast. It was obvious he never was going to be a really good shortstop. He made too many errors, particularly throwing, even though he had a fine arm."

In the schoolboy leagues, and even in Ban Johnson League games, Mantle had appeared to be an adequate shortstop. But the superior caliber of minor-league competition exposed him as being less than satisfactory at that position. In fact, Mantle's erratic throws from shortstop proved so threatening to the paying customers sitting behind first base that team management installed a chicken-wire screen along the first base line.

But that was only part of Mantle's problem. The seventeen-year-old Oklahoman was unable to bear his mistakes, either at the bat or in the field, without becoming violently out of sorts.

"His real weakness," said Craft, "was his temperament. He acted as if the world was coming to an end just because he booted one or struck out in the clutch."

When Mantle messed up, he would vent his anger by kicking dugout water coolers. Once a kick from his spiked shoe caused a water cooler to spring a leak, which unleashed plumes of water and sent his teammates scattering.

The folks back home would have been surprised at such volatility, for the Mickey Mantle his Oklahoma neighbors knew was ever Mutt's shy and unassuming boy. But the hidden pressures that had made Mickey a bed-wetter right up until he began his minor-league career—at Independence, curiously enough, he stopped—still existed. Now, in his eagerness to succeed, those pressures incited the latent rage that drove Mantle's quest for big-league success. And no water cooler was safe from it.

His teammates at Independence kidded him about his temper. Mantle accepted it in the spirit it was intended. He felt at ease with this locker room camaraderie and soon was hanging out with his teammates after the games. Mantle would liken the fraternal bonding of the players—and the experiences they shared—to being back in high school. And in truth it wasn't much different. Where in Commerce Mickey and the guys would hang out at the local pool hall, here in Independence Mantle and his teammates lingered in a luncheonette with the aptly small-town name of "Pop's Place." Afterward, with their bellies filled, they would loiter on the sidewalk in front of "Pop's," joking around and appraising the single girls who came strolling by.

Years later Mantle would say, "Some people are leaders and some are followers. I'm a follower."

That was true enough. In the minors, and later with the Yankees, Mickey seemed drawn to self-assured "action" guys, teammates who liked to party and were aggressive in pursuit of their pleasures. This, like so many aspects of Mantle's behavior, seemed an inevitable outgrowth of his relationship with Mutt. As a child and later as an adolescent, Mickey had been the dutiful son used to following orders. The psyche that evolved was not geared for taking the initiative but rather for following the cues of others.

In Independence, Mantle's leader was third baseman Lou Skizas. Skizas was quick-witted, an extrovert, and a smooth talker. He'd graduated from the University of Illinois with honors. As Mantle recalled: "What a character. The nervous Greek—a pre-fifties hippie from the streets and alleys of Chicago. He [Skizas] had a girl under his arm before and after every game."

For the painfully shy Mantle, Skizas was a man to lead him to the good times that on his own Mickey would not have been able to find. Skizas was at ease chatting up the girls, or kibitzing with teammates.

But though Skizas had a knack for merriment, in a small town such as Independence there wasn't a whole lot of excitement to find. In fact, the life of a bush-leaguer, circa 1949, tended toward the tedium of long bus rides and early wake-up calls in cheap hotel rooms as the team traveled the K-O-M circuit of obscure baseball outposts such as Ponca City and Chanute and Bartlesville and Carthage. None of your bright lights and strutting women in slit dresses here. No, Mantle would get used to dressing out of rusty iron lockers on splintered wooden floors, to night games in poorly lit ballparks, to trying without success to eat on a $2.25 daily meal allowance. To keep from getting stir-crazy, the players played cards, read, told jokes, sang (Mantle's preference was Hank Williams' songs), and sometimes initiated the usual adolescent hijinks of water pistol fights or food fights.

➴ ✦ ➴

"I believe that Mantle is our biggest prize . . ."

Independence would win the K-O-M title in Pittsburg, Kansas, and come back home in the wee hours to celebrate by hooting and hollering and dancing on the empty main drag of the town, with Skizas singing a stirring rendition of "Long Gone Lonesome Blues," a favorite song of Mantle's. The celebration went on until an Independence police officer wandered onto the scene and threatened to bust the noisy celebrants. But the local police quickly backed off when Craft advised him this was a championship celebration.

For Mantle, his first season in organized baseball was a good one: He batted .313 in 89 games, with 7 home runs and 63 runs batted in (RBIs). But his 47 errors at shortstop were a problem

◆ HARRY CRAFT ◆

Harry Francis Craft was born in Ellisville, Mississippi, in 1915.

By the time he was twenty-two years old, the 6 foot, 1 inch tall, 185 pound Craft had made it to the big leagues as an outfielder with the Cincinnati Reds.

Craft lasted six seasons with the Reds, twice as starting centerfielder on pennant winners—the 1939 team, which lost to the Yankees in the World Series, and the 1940 team, which beat Detroit to become world champions. His last year at Cincinnati was in 1942. He finished his major-league playing career with a .253 lifetime batting average.

When Mantle played for him at Independence and later at Joplin, he viewed the manager as a sound baseball man with a real knack for teaching his players.

While managing at Independence, Craft was separated from his wife and in the midst of divorcing her. That left him plenty of free time to dally with other women, which, his players noted, he did on a regular basis. Craft was a meticulous dresser and good-looking, so he tended to have women all along the K-O-M circuit, a social life that made him the envy of his players.

That Craft took his social life seriously was underscored when Skizas happened to intercept a woman who'd come to the Darby Hotel intending to see Craft. When the manager found out she'd been with Skizas, he referred to it obliquely at the ballpark during a team meeting the next night. Without being specific, he spoke of a violation of "a sacred golden rule" and warned that the young man who was guilty of the violation would be wise never to repeat it.

Craft's managerial work in the minor leagues was solid enough to earn him later jobs in the big leagues. From 1957 to 1959 he managed the Kansas City Royals. In 1961, when the Chicago Cubs used a rotating platoon of coaches, Craft was one of them. The following season, he began a three-year managerial stint with the Houston Colt '45s, from 1962 to 1964.

During his seven seasons as a major-league manager, Craft never had a team that played .500 ball or better.

that would give the Yankee organization serious reservations about Mantle's suitability for that position.

But Craft saw the kid from Commerce as a bona fide prospect and alerted the Yankee organization to his potential. For Mantle and his teammates, Craft was something of an enigmatic figure—a shrewd baseball man who conveyed the game expertly but let his players get only so close to him. Mantle would put it this way: "As wonderful and great as he was with his players, nevertheless we'd find it hard to penetrate the inner workings of his mind. A very quiet, cold kind of guy."

Yet Craft had capably filled the void that Mutt's absence had created for Mickey. He might not have been a warm and fuzzy sort of man—neither was Mutt—but he eased Mantle through the rough patches of his first year in the minor leagues. He calmed him when Mickey's temper got the best of him and imparted diamond nuances that would serve Mantle as he moved up in organized baseball. Craft's manner was minimalist and seemingly detached. But Mantle and his teammates recognized that the manager had their best interests at heart.

When the season ended, Mantle went back to Oklahoma to work in the mines at $33 a week. Mutt was by now a ground boss at Blue Goose Number One, earning $75 a week and in a position to install his son in a relatively easy above-ground job.

That November Mantle was summoned to appear by his draft board, a notice that alarmed Mutt and his son for the crimp it could throw in their plans for a big-league future. But the military took a look at the X rays Mantle brought with him and decided that with his history of osteomyelitis Mantle was unfit for military duty. He was classified as 4-F.

Just before the New Year, Mantle began dating a high school majorette from Picher named Merlyn Johnson. Merlyn

Craft (center) eventually managed in the major leagues. Here he is seen with Rusty Staub (right) and an unidentified player during his years in Houston.

was a pretty girl, who, like Mantle, was shy, confessing to be ill at ease in crowds and withdrawn around strangers. Her family was in the lumber business and, by contrast to the mining community, was better off financially.

When Mantle would pick up Merlyn for a date, it would be in the two-toned 1947 Chevrolet Fleetline with mohair seats and vacuum shift that he'd bought with his bonus money and they'd spend their nights at the movies or necking. In her senior year at Picher, Merlyn won a scholarship to a junior college in Miami, Oklahoma. She had ambitions to be a singer.

"But," she said, "once Mickey Mantle came into my life, I forgot about anything else . . . I just fell hard for Mickey."

In February 1950, Mickey and other minor leaguers were invited to a Yankee instructional school in Phoenix, in advance of spring training. The team's manager, Casey Stengel, and his coaching staff were on hand to look over the minor-league talent. When baseball commissioner Happy Chandler got wind of the school he ordered that it be disbanded, since it jumped the gun on the March 1 starting date for spring training. But while the seminar lasted, Mickey made a lasting impression on Stengel:

"We had all kinds of infielders there, like [Gil] McDougald, who was a second baseman then, and [Jerry] Coleman, who was my second baseman in the World Series, and [Billy] Martin, who was a shortstop then. This kid [Mantle] is just standing behind 'em all in practice, like a scavenger, being timid and just shagging balls which gets away from the others. He kept his head down, like his shoes was gonna fall off or somethin' and blushed when you talked to him.

"Being so shy wasn't remarkable, seein' as he was only eighteen, but if he wasn't fielding balls, what could you tell about him? Finally we have sprint races and Mantle wins all the time, looking back over his shoulder to see what was keepin' the others. And also he hits the ball out of sight, right handed and left handed, just like he does now."

By the time the Yankees' spring training came around, the Yankee organization was talking in superlatives about the kid from Commerce.

Stengel declared, "I believe that Mantle is our biggest prize, and that he is the number one kid ballplayer in the professional game."

Bill Dickey, a no-nonsense Hall of Fame catcher, told Yankee outfielder Tommy Henrich at spring training: "Tom, you should see this kid Mantle. . . . I've never seen power like that. He hits the ball and it stays hit. He's really going to be something."

Mantle was assigned to the Joplin Miners, a Class C team in

the Western Association. His monthly salary was bumped up to $250, and he was happy to learn that Skizas and others from the Independence team had been promoted to Joplin, too. So had Harry Craft, who would be Mantle's manager once again. When the season began, Mantle, now a muscular 170 pounds, pounded the ball—his home runs sometimes carried beyond the right field fence and through the upper stories of an orphanage. When Joplin played at home, the orphans gathered at the windows to watch the game and await Mantle's next blast. Once, after he drove one through a window, the children hung out a sign saying: THANKS FOR THE BALL, MICKEY!

The home runs Mantle hit drew testimonials around the league from old-time observers who swore that this shot, and that one, by The Mick were the longest home runs they'd ever seen. Mantle was a big reason why the Joplin Miners had by far the best regular-season record in their league, although they did lose in the postseason playoffs. Mickey batted .400 for much of the season, ending with a .383 average, 26 home runs (14 right handed and 12 left handed), and 136 RBIs. But his 55 errors were sufficient cause for Craft to dash off another advisory to Yankee brass suggesting they seriously consider converting Mantle to a third baseman or an outfielder.

The way Mantle was hitting the ball, the Yankee organization was ruminating on how best to harness all that power for the parent team. The club's general manager, George Weiss, had been following Mantle's progress and already was penciling him in for a Yankee Stadium future. Weiss, a graduate of Yale University, had taken a very un–Ivy League course by shooting for a career in baseball—first as a high school coach, then as a promoter of exhibition games that sometimes featured major leaguers such as Ty Cobb and Walter Johnson, and eventually, in 1919 at age twenty-five, as the owner of an Eastern League franchise in New Haven.

By 1932 Weiss had caught the eye of Yankee owner Jake Ruppert, who hired him to run the team's minor-league system. It was Weiss who would press Ruppert to sign a San Francisco Seal named Joe DiMaggio in 1934. Although the Yankee farm system became renowned for the talent it generated, Weiss did it with a budget-minded approach, paying as little as he could for his minor-league operations. That tightfisted mentality would make him the scourge of Yankee players, including Mantle, once Weiss began negotiating contracts as New York's general manager, beginning in 1948.

But in 1950, the grudge that would develop between penny-pinching Weiss and Mantle was a ways off. Mantle was one of many minor-league stars in the Yankee firmament. One day that summer, in the lavish bar and lounge under the stands just to the right of home plate at Yankee Stadium, Weiss told a group of reporters: "We have some fine kids on our farm teams. There's Bill Skowron, the Purdue football player. He's at Norfolk and can hit the ball a mile. Bob Cerv is the longest hitter in the American Association, with Kansas City. And here's a name for you to remember: Mickey Mantle. He's a shortstop with our Joplin club in the Western Association. A switch-hitter with good power. We don't know whether he's a shortstop or not, but he can hit. And he's only eighteen. . . ."

The Yankees rewarded Mantle for his superior season at Joplin by bringing him up to the parent team for the final weeks of the 1950 season as a nonroster player. On September 17, 1950, Mantle would begin to travel with the club, work out before the actual games, and dress alongside players who comprised the best team in baseball.

In 1950 the Yankees would win the American League pen-

George Weiss, general manager of the Yankees.

nant by three games over the Detroit Tigers and then would sweep the Philadelphia Phillies in four games in the World Series. Mantle was in awe of these men, particularly of the great DiMaggio, who had a kind of patrician reserve. The situation became more bearable when the Yankees brought up Skowron, a $25,000 bonus baby, as another nonroster player. The two minor leaguers hit it off, rooming together on the road and at the Concourse Plaza Hotel, near Yankee Stadium, in the Bronx.

When the season ended, Mantle returned to Oklahoma and a job in the mines at $1.25 an hour. And he was back with Merlyn, the relationship getting serious enough for them to discuss a future together. Merlyn had graduated from high school and was working in the accounting department of the First State Bank in Picher. Mutt, who seemed more run-down than Mickey ever remembered him, lobbied for Mantle to marry the girl, saying he wouldn't mind having a freckle-faced grandson to play with. Beyond that, Mutt, a small-town guy to the core, was suspicious about what might happen to his Mickey if some big-city girl got her hooks into him.

⬧ ⬧ ⬧

"Stratmosphere my eye!"

When New Year 1951 arrived, Mantle received a letter from the Yankees instructing him to report to spring training in Phoenix in mid-February. Mantle continued working in the mines, waiting for the team to send him his train ticket. Day after day he went to the mailbox. No ticket. Meanwhile, the Yankees' farm director, Lee MacPhail, was trying to contact Mantle to ask why he wasn't in Phoenix. Mickey didn't realize the Yankees expected to reimburse his travel expenses when he arrived there.

Then one day a sportswriter and photographer from the *Miami Daily News Record* appeared at the mine and told Mantle that MacPhail was trying to get hold of him. The trouble was that the Mantles did not have a phone at the house in Whitebird. The photographer took a shot of Mantle in his miner's gray overalls and cap, smiling through his smudged face. The reporter quoted him as saying he didn't have his train ticket yet. The next day Tom Greenwade appeared with the ticket and expense money.

The Mantle who arrived in Phoenix was, it turned out, worth waiting for. The sound of the ball rocketing off his bat was, as Ted Williams later would describe it, like an explosion. By now Mantle was man-sized, with bulging Popeye-

Mantle saw his first big-league action in 1950.

THE COMMERCE COMET:
SPEED TO BURN

Even though the reports that tracked Mantle's progress in the Yankee farm system always credited him with having excellent speed, the team's brass were stunned when they saw with their own eyes the extent of The Mick's quickness.

Of that 1950 instructional school in Phoenix, Bill Dickey would recall, "When Mantle was playing short he didn't impress me as being particularly fast, but when we divided the boys up for a series of seventy-five-yard sprints, Mickey finished first in his group, looking over his shoulder at the others. Then we had a sprint for the winners and he won that, too. Then he got sick and explained that he wasn't in shape!"

In spring training 1951 Stengel watched Mantle outrun rookies Al Pilarcik and Tom Sturdivant, who were thought to be Mantle's equal in speed. Mickey left them in the dust, and, when Yankee coaches thought it might be a fluke, he did it again.

Stengel was so pleased he demanded that the coaches time Mantle as he raced around the bases. When he was clocked at just under thirteen seconds, Casey had him do it again and again, as though Mantle's superior speed was for his personal pleasure.

Later, when Mantle made it to the major leagues, Lou Miller, a *New York World-Telegram & Sun* sportswriter, clocked him at 3.1 seconds over the 90 feet to first base.

Miller would say that no other left handed hitter he had timed over a two-year period had done better than 3.4 seconds, and that included such noted speedsters as Gil Coan of the Washington Senators, Bill Bruton and Sam Jethroe of the Milwaukee Braves, and Duke Snider of the Brooklyn Dodgers. (In 1950 and 1951 Jethroe led the National League in stolen bases, and from 1953 to 1955 Bruton had that honor.)

When Dickey heard of Miller's findings he told newsmen: "You should time him on his way to second, when he's really moving. Nobody who ever lived can reach second base from the plate as quickly as Mickey Mantle."

It wasn't long before Mantle's speed prompted the sportswriters to tag him "The Commerce Comet."

style forearms, broad shoulders, and a back rippling with muscles. His wide, compact torso meant that his strike zone was not as liberal as it would be for those power hitters who stood 6 feet or taller. That spring, Mantle's drives soared like golf balls. Some doubters attributed the distance of their orbiting flights to the thin air of Arizona.

That got Stengel agitated.

"All I hear from you guys," he said, "is talk about the stratmosphere"—his word. "All I can say is the rest of these guys are hitting in the same air as this kid, and they ain't knockin' balls over the fences the way he is. Stratmosphere my eye! Mantle just hits hard, and you'll see that when we play in other places."

For all his power and speed, Mickey Mantle presented the Yankees with a dilemma: What position to play this phenom, as Stengel had taken to calling him?

Stengel would recall: "I had Rizzuto at short and you couldn't ask for anybody better than that little guy then, could you? And besides, how did we know how much longer the big guy [DiMaggio] was going to play?"

DiMaggio had been a Yankee since 1936, when as a twenty-one-year-old phenom he had batted .323 with 29 home runs and 132 RBIs. He had missed the war years between 1943 and 1945, and experienced an injury-shortened season (76 games) in 1949. But in his twelfth season as a Yankee, in 1950, Joltin' Joe had come back strongly with a .301 average, 32 home runs, and 122 RBIs—impressive statistics for a thirty-five-year-old player.

But there was no telling with a player of his age when the body would begin to break down. To Stengel, Mantle seemed to be just the man to groom as DiMaggio's eventual replacement. As Tommy Henrich, the retired Yankee rightfielder known as

"Old Reliable," began tutoring Mantle in Phoenix in the nuances of outfield play, Stengel, a former major-league outfielder for fourteen years, would observe them and then add his own advice.

When Mantle had turned up at spring training, the Yankees had figured on giving him another season or two of minor-league experience. Mantle figured if he had to do more time in the minors, he hoped it would be with the man who had guided him so skillfully at Independence and Joplin—his old manager, Harry Craft. Craft was now managing the Yankees' AA farm team in Beaumont, Texas. But as the days passed, and Mantle kept hitting at a .400 clip while belting home runs that soared long distances, it began to seem as if Mantle might be good enough to jump straight from Class C to the big show, unlikely as that sounded.

Stengel told newsmen: "That young fellow in the outfield has me terribly confused, and he's getting me more so every day. He should have a year of Triple-A ball under his belt, but you writers have blowed him up so much. . . ."

❖ ❖ ❖

"It's the law of mathematical progression."

But even as Stengel was, in his way, professing his pleasure in Mantle's progress, and even as the team shipped one rookie after another back to the minor leagues, Mantle hadn't yet imagined that he might end up on the Yankee roster when the season began.

That began to change when the Yankees broke training

camp in Phoenix and headed to the West Coast for a series of ten games in northern and southern California. Mantle, McDougald, and pitcher Tom Morgan were the only remaining rookies still with the team. As brilliant as Mantle had been in Phoenix, he outdid himself on the California swing, hitting a barrage of long-distance home runs.

One of Mantle's best shots came as a lefthanded batter at Wrigley Field in Los Angeles. The ball soared up and against a red-brick building in the right-centerfield stands, a spot that only Babe Ruth and a few others had been able to reach.

While the Yanks were in Los Angeles, Branch Rickey, Pittsburgh's general manager, sat next to Yankee co-owner Dan Topping at one of New York's exhibitions and handed him a blank check, telling Topping to fill in the amount it would take for Rickey to land Mantle for the Pirates. While the gesture was a theatrical one, in character for Rickey, it nonetheless under-scored the impact Mantle was having on baseball men.

Others reacted as strongly to the rookie from Oklahoma. When the Yankees played an exhibition game against the University of Southern California on the USC campus, Mantle hit two homers, a triple, and a single, and was mobbed after-ward by students as he tried to board the Yankee bus.

Stengel by now was arguing with General Manager George Weiss to promote Mantle to the Yankee varsity. As he told newsmen: "I been in this here league"—the Pacific Coast League— "myself for a few years. I never seen balls hit like that. This boy is the best switch-hitter that ever lived."

Mantle's heroics made him *the* story of spring training. Not that that was so unusual. The emergence of a hot rookie at spring training was practically a newspaper staple. Some of those heralded prospects would live up to their advance billing and go on to enjoy successful major-league careers. Others would tail off and never be heard from again. But for that moment, at least, the public would know them.

In the case of Mantle, the juxtaposition of his name against DiMaggio's made him hard to forget, even as it set up great expectations among Yankee supporters and gave Mickey his first involvement with the powerful New York press. The publicity had reverberations back in Oklahoma, where folks reading about the eighteen-year-old phenom began wondering why such a fine specimen wasn't in the military while others, less imposing physically, were being inducted and sent to Korea. How could this rascal Mantle be 4-F?

Nearly a year before, in June 1950, North Korea had invaded South Korea. Within days, U.N. forces, dominated by American troops, rallied to South Korea's side. Now, as the Yankees made a right turn and headed back across the country, the war in Korea was intensifying, as was the pressure on Mantle's draft board in Oklahoma.

The Yankees made their way through Texas on toward Kansas City, where Mantle was excused by Stengel so he could be reexamined by the military. Mutt met him at the train depot in Kansas City and accompanied him back to Oklahoma. Mutt looked a bit drawn, Mantle thought on seeing him, but his father shrugged it off, claiming to be in the pink of health.

"I felt relieved," Mantle said. "But still you gotta know how it was. Any outward display of affection between us would have been considered a sign of weakness. . . . I had so many chances then to tell him he was the greatest guy in the world. But everything was left unspoken."

Early in April, a military medical board in Tulsa rejected Mantle again because of the osteomyelitis.

Now Mantle had to clear George Weiss. The Yankee general manager still believed Mantle was too young, too inexperienced, to be in the major leagues. Stengel disagreed, although even he was ready to concede how improbable was the leap Mantle was about to undertake.

As the Yankee manager told reporters: "You writers have blowed him up so much that I have to take him to New York. I'm not blaming you—he's everything you say he is—but it doesn't figure that he's ready. Then again, nothing he does figures."

In the Yanks' final exhibition game, against the Brooklyn Dodgers at Ebbets Field, Mantle got four hits, including a home run that cleared the thirty-eight-foot-high scoreboard in rightfield, 344 feet from home plate, and left him with a spring training batting average of .402 and 9 home runs.

A few days later, the Yankees signed Mantle to a major-league contract worth $7,500 for the 1951 season.

If it wasn't pressure enough to be nineteen and relatively inexperienced, the Yankees now cranked it up another notch, announcing that Mantle would wear the number 6 on his pin-striped jersey. There was no accident in the team's choice of that numeral.

As Yankee publicist Red Patterson said, "It's the law of mathematical progression. Babe Ruth wore number 3 and was succeeded by Lou Gehrig, who wore number 4. Gehrig was succeeded by Joe DiMaggio, who wears number 5. . . ."

The message was crystal clear: The Yankees were expecting nothing short of greatness from Mickey Charles Mantle.

circa 1951

CHAPTER THREE

ROOKIE YEAR

H ard on a spring of heroic baseball, the nineteen-year-old Oklahoman, a simple country boy, was a New York Yankee. As Stengel said, it didn't figure. Yet here he was, Mutt's kid, making his bid for baseball legitimacy far in advance of expectations.

But with this golden opportunity came enormous pressure. The morning after the Yankees pulled into Grand Central Station in New York for their opening game against the Boston Red Sox, Dan Parker, a popular sports columnist with the *New York Daily Mirror*, wrote: "If the inking device on the Fordham University seismograph didn't trace a design like a cross section of Mount Everest set in the middle of the American prairies . . . it's a fraud because . . . Mickey Mantle, the rookie of the aeons, hit New York like fifteen simultaneous earthquakes."

Branch Rickey told newsmen: "Mantle is the finest

prospect I've ever seen. He's the kind of kid I've always dreamed of finding but never have."

Even his teammates let Mantle know they were counting on him. On the taxi ride from Grand Central Station to the Concourse Plaza Hotel, where Mantle and other Yankees stayed, the cab rolled past Yankee Stadium, prompting relief pitcher Joe Page to nudge Mantle and say, "There it is, phenom! Take a good look 'cause that's The House That Ruth Built. And you're gonna tear it down with your hitting."

Unlike McDougald and Morgan, the other rookies who had made the Yankee team, Mantle was the spotlighted one, his every move a cause for observation, speculation, and potential adulation. When Stengel announced that Mantle would be starting in rightfield on Opening Day, it set off a frenzy of media activity. As Mantle would recall: "Writers, photographers, and broadcasters came at me from every direction. I wanted to run away and hide."

As he walked into Yankee Stadium for that first game, Mantle certainly felt vulnerable, for he knew that his every move would be closely scrutinized and that his margin for error—given the expectations he had raised with his glorious play in spring training—was virtually nil.

As he would later say: "The baseball writers pulled out all the stops. Some even had me ticketed for the Hall of Fame before I had taken my first swing in a major-league game."

On Opening Day, Mantle got to the clubhouse early and, like a child sneaking a peek at the Christmas tree, checked out the lineup sheet. Jackie Jensen, the leftfielder, was leading off. Rizzuto at shortstop was batting second. And there *he* was— Mantle, batting third and playing rightfield. The rest of the lineup showed DiMaggio in centerfield, batting fourth. Yogi Berra, catcher, fifth. Johnny Mize, first base, sixth. Gil

McDougald, third base, seventh. Jerry Coleman, second base, eighth. And pitching and batting ninth, the Springfield Rifle, Vic Raschi.

Mantle, Jensen, and DiMaggio as the outfield prompted sports columnist Red Smith to observe that it was an outfield "with 17 years of major league experience, 16 of which belong to DiMaggio." Even that was an oversimplification, for while it was DiMaggio's 1,621st major-league game, it was Jensen's 46th and Mantle's first.

Finally, it was time to head for the field. As he stepped out of the dugout, Mantle saw the curving triple-tiered grand-stands of the stadium and heard the electric hum of 45,000 baseball fans awaiting the start of another season. Forty-five thousand people—twenty times the population of Commerce.

"I was just plain scared," Mantle said. "All I could think about was that Ted Williams was the greatest lefthanded pull hitter in the business and that he might sock a ball that I could not handle."

Well, the rookie fears were unfounded. Not only did Mantle catch a skybuster of a fly ball from Williams that afternoon, but also, in the sixth inning, he got his first big-league base hit, a line-drive single between short and third that would score Jensen in the Yankees' Opening Day victory.

Nothing Mantle did that afternoon discouraged the roseate visions the baseball press had of him. After the game, reporters approached DiMaggio for his perspective on Mantle.

"The kid was all right," he said. "I appreciate what he is going through. I had played before large crowds in the Pacific Coast League before I came to the Yankees, but Yankee Stadium is something special and don't ever let anybody tell you different."

A day after the Yankees' opening game, the hard-boiled

columnist for the *New York Journal-American*, Jimmy Cannon, would write: "I'm all out of breath hollering it up for this kid."

Tom Meany in *Collier's Magazine* declared: "There seems no doubt that Mantle is destined for eventual stardom in Yankee Stadium."

Meanwhile, the Yankees were doing their best to make Mantle's transition from Class C to the big leagues as smooth and as painless as possible. Berra, for instance, warned him to beware of an umpire named Bill McGowan, who liked to test rookies by calling a really bad pitch a strike. Berra told Mantle not to react when McGowan baited him. Mantle did just as Yogi said when McGowan called a pitch that was way wide of the plate a strike. Mantle looked straight ahead and showed no reaction. For the rest of his career, Mantle would get along just fine with McGowan.

Of particular concern to the Yankees was Mantle's inexperience as an outfielder. Stengel had asked DiMaggio in center to

Two of the greatest Yankees ever—Joe DiMaggio and Mickey Mantle.

serve as a watchdog for Mantle. By shouted direction, "The Yankee Clipper," as DiMaggio was known, would move Mantle into position for the various batters. When a ball was hit toward Mantle, DiMaggio would "talk" him into the catch, much in the manner of a flight controller "talking" a pilot into a landing. When fly balls soared toward right-center, DiMaggio often would let Mantle make the catch on a ball he could have caught as easily, to build the rookie rightfielder's confidence.

❦ ❦ ❦

"New York was a nightmare for me in the beginning."

That was why when New York played its first series in Boston, against the Red Sox, Stengel decided to bench Mantle. Rightfield in Fenway Park, the Red Sox home field, was tricky going for a veteran outfielder, much less a "green pea" such as Mantle. Fenway's rightfield was a wide expanse whose difficulty was compounded by a glaring sun and often gusting wind.

"I don't want to put any additional pressure on the boy," said Stengel. "He never wore sunglasses until a couple of weeks ago. In my opinion he's a big-leaguer right now, but he has the handicap of having to learn a new position."

There were pressures beyond the playing field with which newcomer Mantle would struggle, too. New York was a big city, a glittering, diverse place, especially in comparison to provincial Commerce. For a young man as ingenuous as Mantle, it was a puzzle to figure out how to adjust to the fast-paced, fast-track urban life.

"New York," Mantle recalled, "was a nightmare for me in

the beginning. I guess it figured to be for any country boy. The people seemed strange. They didn't talk like the easygoing folks back home, and I found it hard to understand them. They didn't understand me, either."

The people with whom he had the hardest time communicating were the press. While Mantle was a *cause célèbre* to the beat writers covering the team, they had hoped he would be quotable in the bargain. But Mantle was ill at ease with the hurly-burly of big-time baseball coverage. As the media capital of the world, New York offered readers seven dailies to choose from and in 1951 baseball was a "hot" topic in New York. The city was in the midst of what, in retrospect, would be regarded as a golden age of baseball. There were two extraordinary teams in the National League, the New York Giants and the Brooklyn Dodgers, and the Yankees, of course, remained the most successful team in baseball. The coverage was extensive and competitive.

For a rookie in the spotlight, the rites of news-gathering could be a bit baffling. "I never was very handy with words and I'd always been a little shy among strangers," Mantle said. "I could say things that needed saying, but if a 'yes,' 'no,' or 'maybe' filled the bill, I never bothered saying much else. In the big leagues I began to learn that those weren't good answers. The shyness was misunderstood. Some thought I was surly or conceited."

There is no crime, certainly, in being inarticulate, or even in being indifferent to the attentions of the press. But for the rest of his career, Mantle's coexistence with the writers would prove to be a largely thorny one. At this point, in 1951, Mantle was simply uneasy with the protocol of the interview. As the years wore on and as Mantle gained a degree of sophistication, there would sometimes be malice aforethought in The Mick's dealings with the press.

In '51, the press that covered Mantle found him a difficult interview, and some of the reporters mentioned it to Stengel. The Yankee manager wasn't troubled by that. In the end, Mickey Mantle would be judged on whether he could live up to the Yankee tradition of excellence.

By Yankee tradition, ballplayers were supposed to look and act like major leaguers. That meant an image of a clean-cut and upright athlete—a model for the generation of youngsters who idolized baseball players. While that was the goal, the goal did not always hold. It was a rare ballclub that hadn't a lush or a lout, maybe even several of them, in its midst. With the Yankees, nobody had been a bigger hell-raiser than Babe Ruth, who ate, drank, and chased women, all to excess.

Still, the idea existed that a ballplayer ought to appear to be a gent, at least when he was in public view. That was why, when Yankee outfielder Hank Bauer saw how the team's highly publicized rookie was dressed early in the season, the ex-Marine decided to be Mantle's fashion arbiter. One look at Mantle's threadbare sports coat, the wide tie with the painted peacock, and the Hush Puppies was all Bauer needed to decide a makeover was in order. The next day he brought Mantle to a downtown clothier frequented by Yankee players, and Mantle walked away a new man sartorially, the proud possessor of two moderately priced sharkskin suits, new shirts, ties, and a pair of dress shoes.

But though Mantle had the *look* now of a Yankee, he had not lost his hayseed susceptibility. Alone in New York, he was still a stranger in a strange land—nineteen years old and none too wise to big-city ways. And that would lead to Mantle's involvement in a business relationship he would have been better off avoiding.

Allan Savitt—a man described by one publication as "a

YANKEE TRADITION

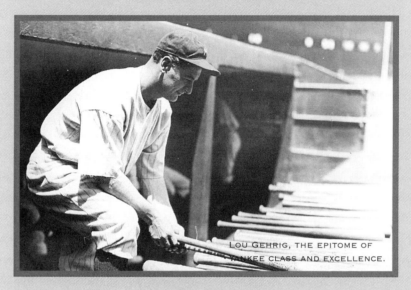

LOU GEHRIG, THE EPITOME OF
YANKEE CLASS AND EXCELLENCE.

In the beginning, back at the turn of the century, the American League team from New York was known as the Highlanders because of the location of the club's ballpark, on an elevated parcel of land in the Washington Heights section of Manhattan.

The name "Highlanders" was a mouthful, and cumbersome for newspaper headline writers, so the team came to be known as the "Yankees," officially so in 1913 when it began playing its home games in the Polo Grounds, which the Yankees shared with the more established and successful New York Giants of the National League.

But beginning in the 1920s, the Yankees would outstrip the Giants and every other organization in baseball and establish a Yankee tradition that became synonymous with a first-class operation . . . and victory.

The turning point came in 1920, when Harry Frazee, the owner of the Boston Red Sox, sold pitcher-outfielder George Herman (Babe) Ruth to the Yankees for $100,000. That was considered big money in those times. And Frazee was in desperate need of the cash, not just for his ball club but also for his Broadway musical *No, No, Nanette.*

For the Yankees the hundred grand turned out to be money very well spent. Ruth, who had had back-to-back 20-plus-win seasons as a Red Sox pitcher in 1916 and 1917, turned the Yankees into a winner, playing every day as an outfielder and becoming baseball's first great power hitter. In his inaugural season as a Yankee, in 1920, he hit .376, with 54 home runs, more home runs than any player had ever hit in a season. To get an idea of Ruth's dominance in his time, remember this: The runner-up to Ruth in the American League that year was the St. Louis Browns' George Sisler, who hit 19 home runs. The National League home run leader in 1920 was Cy Williams of the Philadelphia Phillies, with 15 home runs.

But to Yankee fans what mattered most was that The Babe brought respectability to the franchise. With Ruth in the lineup the team began winning, and winning often, through the Roaring Twenties and the Depression thirties. And even after he was traded, in 1935, the Yankees kept on winning. From 1921 through 1950 New York won seventeen American League pennants and thirteen World Series, a record of success that no other franchise had approached.

Through those years the Yankees kept finding great players, and integrating them without a hitch into a ball club that constantly operated as a team. Yes, the Yankees had stars—Ruth, Gehrig, DiMaggio—but the stars functioned within a team concept, and whereas other franchises changed managers like flashlight batteries, stability was a constant in the tradition of Yankee success, with Miller Huggins (1918–1929) and Joe McCarthy (1931–1946) being prime examples.

No team commanded more fear, and loathing, than the Yankees. The organization operated with a business-like efficiency that struck some as being cold and robotic. Yankee *hauteur* made some fans regard them with distaste; the New York Yankees were not a warm, fuzzy team. Yankee-haters—and they were legion—considered the team lucky. It galled them to see other teams' castoffs, such as an aging Johnny Mize or Johnny Sain suddenly spark up and contribute mightily to another Yankee pennant winner.

Yankee fans said that was the mark of a brainy organization. They pointed to the succession of dominant players as being the hallmark of Yankee tradition, a tradition that as the 1951 season unfolded Mickey Mantle was expected to sustain.

small, melancholy individual who wears horn-rimmed glasses"—offered to set up Mantle with a firm that secured testimonials and endorsements for celebrities. The problem with the arrangement was that the split on revenues—50 percent for Mantle and 50 percent for the company representing him—was an inequitable cut for the ballplayer by prevailing standards.

But on April 18 Mantle signed a two-year deal with the company, and nearly a week later signed another contract, a ten-year deal making Savitt his personal representative, at a standard 10 percent, "in the field of radio, television, personal appearances, stories for books and magazines, and all other fields, exclusive of baseball playing. . . ."

Once again, Bauer came to the rescue. When he heard about the unsound business arrangements Mantle had made, he urged Mantle to let the Yankees in on what he had done so they might intervene, perhaps even use their considerable influence to quash the deals. Bauer explained that the 50–50 split exploited him and that the Yankee office could procure endorsements for him, as it had for his teammates, without taking any portion of his money.

The Yankees did step in, and eventually Mantle extricated himself from the onerous contracts, though a lawsuit was later brought by Savitt. The incident was a sobering lesson for Mantle about the vagaries of life in the big city. Mantle would say, "People up here have funny ideas. Everybody's got a different way of making money up here. Down where we live, all we got is mining and a rubber company. I know they're just trying to make a living and I don't blame them. If I were outside of baseball, I suppose I'd be trying to think of some way to do it, too."

At least there was baseball to anchor him. In the early weeks of the season, Mantle was playing up to his press notices. He hit his first major-league home run on May 1, a 450-footer against righthander Randy Gumpert at Comiskey Park in Chicago. A couple of days later, he hit another home run, at Sportsman's Park in St. Louis, that traveled more than 450 feet. Weeks later, he was still going strong, batting .316 with 4 home runs—2 of them right-handed and 2 left-handed—and he was leading the American League in RBIs, with 26.

But then—trouble.

Pitchers got wise to Mantle. They discovered he could be baited into going after the high fastball, just above the letters on the pinstriped jersey. High and tight, up and in.

Mantle began striking out with all too frequent regularity. When he fanned five times in a doubleheader against the Red Sox, he dragged back to the bench after the last strikeout and told Stengel: "Put someone in there who can hit the ball. I can't." Then he sat down on the bench and cried. Against Cleveland's Bob Lemon he struck out three straight times and, head down, stormed into the dugout and smashed two bats against the wall.

❧ ❧ ❧

"I thought I raised a man. You ain't no man."

I reacted like the nineteen-year-old kid I was," Mantle said. "I kicked the cement posts of the dugout so often that my toes were black and blue. And when my toes hurt too much, I'd bust my bat on the dugout steps. The sides of my locker took a pounding whenever I reached the clubhouse still traveling under a full head of steam."

In spite of Mantle's assertion that his outbursts were an adolescent norm, the truth is his behavior was excessive for any age. Assume his public failure was crushing to his ego. Then imagine the injury it did to the cherished dream he'd shared with Mutt. That, more than anything, likely accounted for Mantle's inability to cope with his decline at the bat. The pressure was more than he could handle; the idea of failing his father intensified his anguish.

Nor was the reaction of the Yankee faithful helpful. As the slump deepened, Yankee fans booed him, feeling let down by this "next DiMaggio." He was called a bum, a draft dodger, and some names that were unprintable. Although teammates tried to reassure him, Mantle was coming unglued. The negative reaction of the crowd only made the perfectionist in Mantle press harder. He routinely began swinging at pitches that sailed far and wide of the strike zone, even those thrown into the dirt. He was overanxious and growing more desperate by the day. By mid-June his batting average had dipped to .269.

Stengel began platooning Mantle with Jackie Jensen. By mid-July Mantle had a credible 45 RBIs, but he had struck out 52 times in 246 at-bats and had lost faith in his ability to hit the baseball.

On July 15 Stengel called Mantle into his hotel suite in Detroit and told the rookie he was being sent down to the Kansas City Blues, a Triple-A team in the American Association, subject to recall at twenty-four hours' notice. Mantle's eyes filled with tears.

"I felt like running off and hiding someplace where there was no baseball," he later recalled. "Perhaps it wouldn't have been as hard to take if there had been no ballyhoo. But now the big bubble had burst and I felt I was the laughingstock of the league. The same newspapers that billed me as a superstar in April were now saying I was through."

Stengel and the Yankees were hoping that, removed from the pressure of a big-league setting and batting now against American Association pitchers, Mantle would retool his swing, regain his confidence, and be the phenom he had been in the spring. As soon as the Yankees saw Mantle was back in the groove, they were prepared to restore him to their roster.

But Mantle was so distraught from his demotion that he continued to struggle in Kansas City. He had become his own worst enemy, allowing his slump to undermine his confidence. Rather than find his hitting stroke against minor-league pitching, he sank further into his dark moods and remained an easy out. In his first twenty-three times at bat for Kansas City he managed only one hit, a bunt single. But even that hit did not satisfy Kansas City manager George Selkirk, who told Mantle he had not been sent down to the American Association to practice bunting. The Yankees wanted him to be the hitter they knew he could be.

Mantle's state of mind by now was so shaky that he contemplated quitting baseball and going back to Oklahoma. Feeling down and miserable, Mickey phoned Mutt at the Eagle-Picher mine and told him how he was struggling. Not that Mutt was unaware of Mickey's slump. He read the box scores and knew his boy was floundering. But he was sure that Mickey would right himself; he thought it was only a matter of time. Then came the voice on the long-distance line that made him wonder if he had misjudged his son.

Mutt heard the desperation in his son's voice. Alarmed, he told Mickey to wait in his room at the Aladdin Hotel; he'd be in Kansas City pronto. Mutt left Commerce immediately, arriving after a five-hour drive, looking haggard. But when he demanded that Mickey explain himself, and his son reiterated his feeling that he couldn't cut it as a ballplayer, Mutt immediately grasped that his son was subtly asking his permission to quit.

For Mutt Mantle, the idea of quitting was reprehensible. It squandered all the hard work that father and son had put into their shared dream of baseball glory. Mutt fixed him with a sharp look and began packing Mantle's bags.

"Then," Mantle said, "he says—and this is what got me— he says, 'I thought I raised a man. You ain't no man. You're a coward.' And he's packing my clothes and he's crying. And I started crying. . . . I finally talked him into letting me have one more chance."

As his father climbed back into the old LaSalle for the return trip to Commerce, Mantle—shaken by the encounter— faced the challenge of fighting his slump and showing the Yankees he still could be the ballplayer they envisioned.

In the first game of Kansas City's next series, in Toledo, he came out of his slump with a vengeance. In his first 4 at-bats he hit a double, a triple, and 2 towering home runs. Then, in his final at-bat, he laid down a bunt for a base hit— "going for the cycle." This time Selkirk didn't mind: He winked at Mantle and urged him to keep going like that.

Mantle kept going. After 40 games with Kansas City he had upped his batting average to .361, with 9 doubles, 3 triples, 11 home runs, and 50 RBIs. That was good enough for Stengel, whose team was in a dogfight of a pennant race. The Yanks needed the kind of explosive power Mantle possessed.

But just when New York was about to bring Mantle back to the big leagues again, his draft board intervened, demanding that Mickey report for still another examination, this one at Fort Sill, Oklahoma, on August 23. Once again, he was reject-ed as unfit for military service because of the osteomyelitis. Just the same, the critics and superpatriots continued to depict him as a privileged character and draft dodger.

On August 24 Mantle was recalled by the Yankees and

reissued a uniform, this one with the number 7 on it. This time around, he decided he'd rather not stay in a hotel room, and so he moved into a midtown Manhattan apartment, over the Stage Deli, which he shared with Bauer and Hopp. Even as he was back with the Yankees, restored to the starting lineup, he was beginning to feel like less of a stranger in New York.

❧ ❧ ❧

"It was a lot of fun while it lasted."

The Stage—noted for its thick corned beef and pastrami sandwiches, its matzo-ball soup, and its cheesecake—was owned by Max and Hymie Asnas, who treated Mantle like an adopted son, plying him with cholesterol-laden delicacies the country boy couldn't resist. Sometimes he would meet up for a late-night drink with a chorus girl he liked named Holly. Through her, Mickey rubbed up against the big-city high life; in his words: "meeting Holly's friends, getting stuck with the check at too many fancy restaurants, discovering scotch at too many dull cocktail parties. It was a lot of fun while it lasted."

On the playing field he stepped right back into the Yankees' starting lineup—at least until the final games, when Stengel left him on the bench and went with his veteran players. And while Mantle didn't hit like the spring-training phenom, when he did play, he contributed. New York finished five games ahead of the second-place Cleveland Indians, and Mantle ended up with a .267 batting average, 13 home runs, and 65 RBIs through 96 games.

Mantle was well aware that he had not lived up to his

All of baseball debated whether Mantle or Mays was the better center fielder.

advance notices. Once the season began, other rookies seized the spotlight. His teammate McDougald had been a model of consistency at third base all season, batting .306 and fielding flawlessly. McDougald, not Mantle, would be the American League Rookie of the Year.

In the National League, the Giants' Willie Mays had captivated the baseball world, as much for the gusto with which he played the game as for the all-round talent he possessed. Mays ran out from under his cap to catch fly balls, he slid into bases with reckless abandon. He could hit (.274, 20 home runs, 68 RBIs); he could field. And he was stylish to boot. When fly balls floated out to center, Mays would gather them in, casually, with his glove upturned at his belt buckle—what baseball writers called the basket catch. Mays transmitted a boyish pleasure in playing the game and quickly caught on as "The Say Hey Kid," a favorite of the fans.

Mays's Giants team would provide the opposition for the Yanks in the '51 World Series by coming from 13 games behind and beating their crosstown rival, the Brooklyn Dodgers, in the final game of a best-of-three playoff series. That was the game that ended dramatically when Bobby Thomson hit a three-run home run in the bottom of the ninth to give the Giants a come-from-behind victory.

Mutt Mantle—not content to watch the Series on TV—had decided to drive in from Oklahoma to see the games in person. For the Mantles, Mickey's being in the World Series was a shining moment in their lifelong pursuit of the baseball dream. On the long road to diamond glory, there had been a few bumps along the way. But this made the hard work, and the occasional reversal, worth it. For both Mantles, the Series opener was bound to be a disappointment. Although Mickey drew two walks against the Giants' Dave Koslo, Koslo beat the Yankees, 5–1. Neither Mantle regarded the loss as anything more than a momentary obstacle to Yankee supremacy. The Yankees had a tradition of success, and tomorrow was another day.

So when Mickey arrived at the clubhouse, and Mutt settled into his seat for the second game of the Series, it was in anticipation of happier circumstances.

In the clubhouse, Stengel was already thinking tactically. Even before the game started, he buttonholed Mantle and told him he wanted him to cover for DiMaggio in centerfield and try to get to as many fly balls as he could from rightfield.

"The Dago's heel is hurting pretty bad," Stengel told Mantle. DiMaggio, thirty-six now and obliged to play in pain, had hoped to make '51 a triumphant final year. But the season proved to be a disappointment. DiMaggio's batting average dipped to .263, his lowest ever during his eighteen seasons as a Yankee, and the power he once could generate with his stylish swing vanished, too—12 home runs, whereas the year before he had hit 32 of them.

Alerted to DiMaggio's condition, Mantle made a mental note to be ready to give The Yankee Clipper the sort of backup that DiMaggio had provided him earlier in the season.

Meanwhile, Mantle was helping the Yankees at bat. In the opening inning he got his first World Series base hit when he bunted safely. Rizzuto bunted him to second base, and Mantle then scored on a Texas League single by McDougald to give the Yankees a 1–0 lead.

It was 2–0 by the fifth inning when Mays hit a fly ball to short right-center. Mindful of Stengel's instructions, Mantle started for the ball, intent on catching it and keeping DiMaggio from having to tax himself. But at the last second he heard DiMaggio holler, "I have it," and tried to veer out of his way. As Mantle braked, his spikes caught on the rubber cover of a sprinkler fixture. He went down as if he'd been shot, as DiMaggio reached over the rookie's body and caught the ball. Then DiMaggio bent down to help Mantle.

"I was afraid he was dead," DiMaggio later recalled. "I shouted, 'Mick! Mick!' and he never moved a muscle or batted an eye. Then I waved to our bench to send out a stretcher. . . . After what seemed like a couple of minutes but probably wasn't that long, Mantle suddenly opened his eyes and burst out crying. He bawled like a baby. I don't know whether he thought maybe he had missed the ball or that he was seriously injured."

He was seriously injured—two torn ligaments in his right knee—and had to be carried off the field. By the time he reached the dugout he saw Mutt in the stands.

Mantle's knee was wrapped and splinted by team trainer Gus Mauch, and he left the stadium on crutches. The next morning he took a taxi to Lenox Hill Hospital, where he was scheduled to have the knee operated on. As the cab came to a stop at the 77th Street entrance to the hospital, Mutt got out first, followed by Mickey on crutches. As Mantle readied himself to step up onto the curb, he put his hand on his father's shoulder to steady himself and then shifted his weight onto Mutt, who promptly crumbled to the ground.

"That was the first time I knew Dad was really sick," Mantle said.

Doctors at Lenox Hill placed Mutt in a bed next to his son's as Mickey was prepped for surgery. Even before test results on Mutt's condition came back, Mickey began suspecting the worst. He had viewed his father as forever vigorous, but now he realized he had ignored the signs. When Mutt had turned up in New York for the World Series, his clothes hung loosely about his frame, giving him something of a scarecrow appearance. But Mickey had refused to see that for what it was, deluding himself that Mutt was fine . . . maybe just a bit run-down.

Mantle's knee was surgically repaired and then placed in a special cast that could accommodate steel weights that Mantle was advised to work out with over the winter. As he lay in bed following surgery, there came the knock at his door that Mantle had been fearing. From the look on the doctor's face, he knew the news was bad. The doctor took a deep breath and told him. Mutt Mantle had Hodgkin's disease, and it was an advanced case. His father was dying.

"All that year he was in pain," said Mantle. "He was so sick he couldn't sleep in bed at night, and he used to sit up in a chair. But he wouldn't let my mother tell me he was dying. He just said he had a backache. He figured I was having a hard enough time making the Yankees."

Back to Oklahoma the Mantles went, Mickey to heal, Mutt to live out his final days. With his World Series winning share,

Mantle bought his parents a seven-room house at 317 South River Street in Commerce. It was the first time the Mantles could boast of a house with indoor plumbing.

Then Mantle's thoughts turned to Merlyn. In New York, Mickey had introduced his showgirl to Mutt, who had not been impressed. Mutt had told his son that Merlyn was the woman for him—she was, in his father's phrase, Mickey's "own kind."

Do the right thing, Mutt told him. Marry her.

Two days before Christmas 1951, Mickey Mantle and Merlyn Johnson were married at her parents' home in Picher.

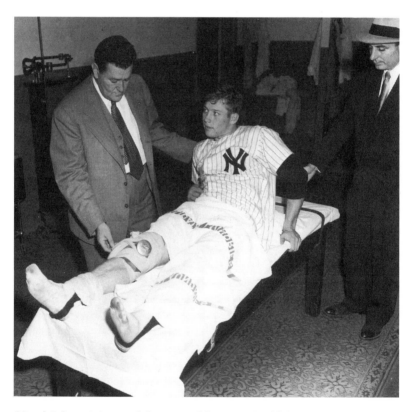

Mantle's knee injury took him out of the 1951 World Series.

Years later, in a book about Mantle published after he died, Merlyn would write:

> I knew that we loved each other. I also knew that marriage was not a real high priority for Mick—he was twenty years old and just starting to live his dream. . . . He was married but in a very small geographic area of his mind.

The honeymoon? Mantle had been led to believe that he had a free weekend arranged in Hot Springs, Arkansas, complete with the bridal suite at a fancy hotel there.

To double the pleasure, Mantle decided to invite another couple—his good friend Bill Moseley, and Moseley's wife. Moseley and he had been teammates on the Commerce High basketball and football teams, and Mantle thought it would be fun for the four of them to enjoy a honeymoon weekend in Hot Springs together.

The trouble was that when the couples arrived in Hot Springs, Mantle discovered that the man who had promised him his gratis lodgings—supposedly a higher-up with the Hot Springs Chamber of Commerce—was a ghost figure. Nobody at the Chamber of Commerce had heard of him, or knew anything about Mantle's complimentary arrangements.

The Mantles and the Moseleys rented their rooms for one night in Hot Springs, had breakfast there the next morning, then drove back to Commerce.

End of honeymoon. Beginning of a marriage.

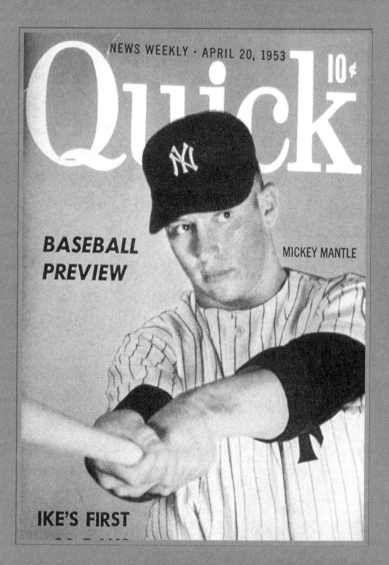

NEWS WEEKLY · APRIL 20, 1953

Quick

10¢

BASEBALL
PREVIEW

MICKEY MANTLE

IKE'S FIRST

circa 1953

CHAPTER FOUR

GROWING PAINS

D iMaggio was gone, retired after the 1951 season.

Who would succeed The Yankee Clipper in centerfield—
Jackie Jensen or Mantle?

Had Mantle taken pains to rehabilitate his knee, it would
have been a no-brainer for Stengel. But over the winter Mickey
had been a slacker, ignoring the regimen of weight exercises
he was advised to do to strengthen his leg. When he reported
to spring training in St. Petersburg, Florida, he was still gimpy
from the World Series mishap. That disregard for doing right
by his natural talent would be chronic during Mantle's baseball career. Though he had the body that any aspirant to the
game would have killed for, Mantle would make a habit of
abusing it over eighteen seasons.

Whether it was a form of rebellion that Mickey—hitherto
the dutiful son—indulged or simply the reflex reaction of a
natural athlete who was convinced of his invincibility, who can

say? What we do know is that years later, The Mick would rue the fact that he did not take pains to care for his body.

"Everything had always come natural to me," he said years later. "When the last World Series game was over, I didn't think about baseball until the spring. I blame that on stupidity."

Given Mantle's physical limitations as the '52 season began, Stengel had no choice but to start Jensen in center and keep the somewhat debilitated Mantle, his right knee heavily taped, in right. The trouble with that solution was that Jensen failed to hit, and the Yankees dropped to sixth place. Two weeks into the season, the Yankees traded Jensen to Washington for Irv Noren, an accomplished center fielder.

On May 6, before a game against the Cleveland Indians, Stengel phoned Mantle at his hotel room to say that Mutt Mantle had died of Hodgkin's disease. Dead at age thirty-nine. When Mantle hung up, there were tears in his eyes and, though he had known for a long time now that his father was terminally ill, still he was inconsolable and angry. Mantle flew to Oklahoma in time to see his father buried in a miners' cemetery alongside Tunney and Grandpa Charlie. When Emmett Mantle, Mutt's other brother, died later that year of Hodgkin's disease, it reinforced Mickey's belief that he was fated to die young too.

"I was the Yankee player representative," Jerry Coleman recalled. "Once, when we were discussing pensions, Mickey said, 'You don't have to talk to me about pensions. I don't think I'm going to be here to collect any.' He laughed when he said it, but I think he meant it. I don't think he believed he'd live to fifty." But flying back to New York to rejoin the team after his father's funeral, Mantle had a sobering sense of his immediate future.

"Up to Dad's death, baseball had been a game," Mantle

said. "Now it was a profession. I had to make good for Mama, for my twin brothers, Ray and Roy, for my sister, Barbara, my kid brother, Larry, and my wife, Merlyn. . . . I had to make it, and I felt that I would. Dad had raised me to be a ballplayer."

Mantle claimed to have been a very occasional drinker while his father was alive. It was when Mutt died that he said he turned to drink as a balm against the pain he felt about his father's premature passing.

"I began to doubt God," Mantle said. "All I knew was a bottomless sorrow, and I couldn't express it to anyone."

That quickly evolved into a pattern of social drinking that became so chronic that Stengel felt obliged to speak to him about moderating his nocturnal habits. But Mantle continued to keep late hours and consume quantities of hard liquor.

"Back then," Mantle said, "I could quit drinking when I went to spring training. I got myself into shape. Then when the season started I went back to drinking again. Billy Martin, Whitey Ford, and me."

Martin was, as Skizas had been, a social navigator for Mantle. The brash and aggressive approach Billy took to baseball carried over to his social side. As a Yankee rookie in 1950, Martin had befriended the regal DiMaggio by boldly approaching him to be part of Joe D's postgame plans. DiMaggio, like Stengel, developed a fondness for the cocksure kid from the West Coast and often let Martin join him when he dined out.

Mantle hit it off with Martin from the start. Joined by Ford, they would become "The Three Amigos" of the Yankees, indulging in the sort of rowdy behavior that would raise eyebrows in the team's front office and prompt Stengel, a kind of father figure to his younger players, to caution them about their late hours. But Stengel—a pretty fair drinker himself—was not really given to policing his players' off-hours.

When Mantle rejoined the team following Mutt's funeral, he continued to be in rightfield. But like Jensen before him, Irv Noren had trouble at bat. So on May 20, Stengel decided that Mantle, bad knee or not, was his centerfielder. As baseball writer Joe Trimble would observe: "Casey knew the chances of a fourth straight pennant—his fanatical desire—depended upon how Mickey came through."

➤ ➤ ➤

"What did you say, Joe?"

That was a lot of pressure to put on an underpaid twenty-year-old. In his second year, Mantle would be playing for the same salary, $7,500, he had earned as a rookie, although his contract came with an incentive clause sweetening his deal by $2,500 if he was still on the Yankee roster in June.

In today's era of soaring multimillion-dollar player salaries, it is a curious footnote to recall that during the '52 season Mantle and Merlyn lived in a tiny room with no stove, refrigerator or television set at the Concourse Plaza Hotel.

"We couldn't afford to rent a television set, at ten dollars a month," said Merlyn. "Mickey needed to send money home to help his family."

Mantle responded to the challenge of being the Yankees' centerfielder. In his first game at that position, against the Chicago White Sox, he had four hits, all singles, which put him over the .300 mark.

As spring turned to summer, Mantle and the Yankees got rolling. The team vaulted into first place, and Mickey continued pounding the baseball. Typical of Mantle's heroics was what he did during a late-season game in Cleveland after

Yankee first baseman Joe Collins hit a home run high into the upper deck in right-center. As Collins crossed home plate and passed Mantle kneeling in the on-deck circle, Collins needled him, saying: "Go chase that, kid."

Mantle stepped up to the plate and drove the pitch higher and deeper into the upper seats than Collins had. As he came into the dugout, he languished over a drink of water before settling onto the bench next to Collins and asking, "What did you say, Joe?"

Mantle would lead the team in hitting in '52, batting .311, third-best in the American League, with 23 home runs and 87 RBIs. With Mantle's hot bat, the Yankees would win their fourth straight American League pennant in a neck-and-neck race with the Cleveland Indians that was not decided until the final week of the season.

And after the disastrous World Series in '51, Mantle's performance against the Dodgers in the '52 Series would prove extremely satisfying to him. With the Dodgers leading three games to two, Mantle hit homers in each of the last two games to help the Yankees rally and win the Series in seven games. In that crucial seventh game, Mickey not only hit a home run off Joe Black but also contributed a savvy fielding play.

Stengel had warned him that Brooklyn's Jackie Robinson would often round first base on a single and bait a throw from the outfielder back to first base, daring him to try to pick him off. But instead of diving back into first base, Robinson would accelerate for second base as soon as the outfielder tipped his throw. In that way he would stretch a routine single into an extra base. So on a three-hop single to right-center, Mantle fielded the ball and *faked* the throw behind Robinson. Robinson went for the fake and lit out for second base.

BILLY MARTIN

TWO OF THE THREE AMIGOS—MICKEY MANTLE AND BILLY MARTIN

If Mantle was so gifted at baseball that he seemed a sure thing for stardom, such was not the case with his good friend Alfred Manuel (Billy) Martin, a.k.a. Alfred Manuel Pesano. Martin was more the self-made player.

Through his hustle and aggression, Martin quickly established himself as a favorite of Yankee manager Casey Stengel, who on occasion would hold up Martin to his teammates as a paragon of what a ballplayer should be.

Martin made just as big an impression on rivals. Cleveland general manager Frank Lane once said of him: "He's the kind of guy you'd like to kill if he's playing on the other team, but you'd like ten of him on your side."

Lane's subtext was that Martin's hard-as-nails attitude compounded what skill he had and made him a fierce competitor—not to mention a winner. Martin would do whatever it took to beat the other guy. Once, when Stengel noticed that Philadelphia Athletics pitcher Harry Byrd scared off Yankee batters with his sidearm deliveries aimed perilously close to them, he offered his players $100 each time any one of them allowed himself to be hit by the pitch that night. Martin went out and got hit by

Byrd's pitches in three different at-bats.

Martin not only had that kind of gutsiness, he also managed to get better the more pressure there was. Once Martin got his chance as a Yankee starter in '52, he demonstrated the ability to perform in clutch situations.

In World Series play Martin was often spectacular. In 28 World Series games he batted .333, in contrast to his lifetime regular-season average of .257. In the 1952 Series, against the Brooklyn Dodgers, Martin gave the Yankees a lift at the bat *and* in the field. In game two, Martin's three-run home run led the Yankees to a 7–1 victory. But it is for his bases-loaded lunging catch of Jackie Robinson's wind-blown infield pop-up late in game seven that he is best remembered from that Series.

The next year, 1953, Martin was the Series' Most Valuable Player, batting .500 with 12 hits, 2 home runs, and 8 RBIs. His single in the bottom of the ninth inning of the sixth game beat the Dodgers and clinched the Yankees' fifth straight World Series triumph. Stengel was so thrilled by Martin's heroics that he rushed out of the Yankee dugout and applied a bear hug on Martin.

Martin missed the '54 season and most of '55 while serving in the military, and the Yankees faltered. Back in the lineup on a regular basis in '56, he played well enough to make the American League All-Star team.

Through his years as a Yankee, Martin acquired a reputation as a combative personality, willing to fight anybody who dared to insult or knock heads with him. Though a man of average size—5 feet, 11½ inches and 165 pounds—Martin was handy with his fists and fearless.

In 1950, when a Red Sox rookie named Jimmy Piersall insulted Martin about the large size of his nose, Martin fought Piersall under the grandstand at Fenway Park in Boston and gave him a beating. Martin did not allow anybody to trifle with him.

But he was equally pugnacious about aggressions committed against teammates, particularly when the Yankees' easygoing shortstop Phil Rizzuto was the target. In one game against the St. Louis Browns, when catcher Clint Courtney intentionally spiked Rizzuto as he slid into second base, Martin immediately came to Rizzuto's defense and began brawling with Courtney. As players from both teams came off their benches and onto the diamond, Martin knocked Courtney's glasses off, and teammate/drinking buddy Whitey Ford stepped on them, smashing them to smithereens.

Mantle's home run in game seven of the 1952 World Series helped clinch the title for the Yankees.

Mantle's clothesline throw to Billy Martin at second base had Robinson by ten to fifteen feet.

Robinson, as smart and daring a player as the game had seen, admired Mantle's cunning enough to tip his hat to Mantle when the umpire called him out at second. After the Series-clinching seventh game, he came by the Yankee clubhouse to compliment him as a player. Mantle, who had a high regard for Robinson, was touched by his gesture.

For Mantle, who had batted .345 (10 for 29) over the seven-game Series, it was a fine finish to a productive season, one that had been an agreeable reversal of his often trying rookie year. Although he played the entire '52 season with an elasticized brace around his right knee, the knee remained intact through the 142 games in which he played. Mantle had played as if in perfect health in spite of the occasional pain. That he had had an impact on the Yankees' success was reflected in his third-place finish in the Most Valuable Player voting of the baseball writers after the season.

Not that there wasn't margin for Mantle to do even better. At the plate, he had struck out 111 times, which gave him the dubious distinction of being the all-time Yankee leader in that category. The previous single-season whiff champion for the franchise had been shortstop Frank Crosetti, who had struck out 105 times in 1937.

Stengel often asked Mantle to cut down on his distinctive go-for-broke swing. The Yankee manager insisted Mantle would be a better hitter if he swung with a foreshortened stroke. But when Stengel advanced such arguments, often with technical fine points that made Mantle instantly blurry-eyed, the Yankee slugger just tuned out. His approach to hitting lacked any in-depth tactical nuances. It was simply hit the bejesus out of the first pitch he could get the wood on. Years later, when baseball folks asked him if he wouldn't have hit for a higher average if he had been more scrupulous about the pitches he swung at, and if he had modified his swing, Mantle would say that if he had wanted to be a career singles hitter like Pete Rose he'd have worn a dress.

Mickey's was a macho approach to the batter's box, and it eventually was part of the charm that made him a legendary Yankee. But it took a while for the legend to be universally accepted. In these early years, Mantle's magnetism as a player—his speed, his power, the very look of him—made him a figure of intrigue to the media. It was a time when athletes tended to be regarded as heroes by the men who wrote and talked about them. Mantle's raw talent—and the more than occasional flashes of his brilliance—surely fascinated the baseball press. But many fans stopped short of embracing The Mick as another DiMaggio. For years, many of them would keep arm's length from Mickey, feeling he had fallen short of that incredible potential. In 1952, everybody from Stengel to the guy in the bleachers had their quibbles about The Mick.

For Stengel, it was not just that herculean swing he wanted to change. It also was Mantle's fitful attention.

"I hafta keep on him," Stengel said. "He seems to drift away from business. I guess I was like that as a kid, too. But he's got the chance for big paydays and he better start to help himself."

Mantle's attention was most apt to falter when he was in the field, particularly after he had failed at bat. The dark temper that Mickey had displayed as a rookie did not abruptly dematerialize.

"He goes out there," said Stengel, "and he's thinking about the last time up and someone hits the ball to him and, oops, he's shocked."

Sometimes Mantle threw to the wrong base, or made a bonehead base-running mistake. Stengel treated him more gingerly than others on the team but still let him know he was dissatisfied.

Just the same, by the 1953 season, the newspapers and mass-circulation magazines had marked The Mick for superstardom. *Time* magazine put Mantle on its cover and referred to him as "Young Man on Olympus."

Collier's featured photos of Mantle's body, and in one that showed his rippling back muscles the magazine captioned: "Here is where the Mantle power comes from. When Mickey first joined the Yankees, manager Stengel called him 'the boy with the man's back.'"

The ballyhoo was substantial, and occasionally Mantle,

now earning an $18,000 salary, gave the public cause to believe he was the phenom of his press clippings. On April 17 in Washington, Mantle hit a shot off the Senators' Chuck Stobbs that cleared the fifty-five-foot-high wall in back of the leftfield bleachers, bounced off a sixty-foot sign some 460 feet from home plate, and came to rest in the backyard of a house just beyond Griffith Stadium. The Yankees' publicity director, Red Patterson, told newsmen he'd measured the distance the ball had carried and announced it as 565 feet. Of course, in later years Mantle said Patterson confessed to him he hadn't ever left the ballpark but rather relied on a PR man's flimflam.

❖ ❖ ❖

"The boy with the man's back"

No matter. The next day's papers not only had stories of the monumental home run—some said it was the longest in baseball history—but also carried diagrams with arrows showing the path of the ball as it left the stadium. Soon after, Mickey's bat and the home run ball were on display at the National Baseball Hall of Fame and Museum in Cooperstown, New York.

Yet as '53 unfolded, Mantle fell short of the grand expectations the media had raised for him. Sure, there were times when he would hit a home run practically into the ionosphere. But consistency was his problem. Injuries didn't help. Mantle sprained his left knee at midseason and then, favoring his "good" knee—the right knee he'd hurt in the '51 World

Series—he tore ligaments in that knee and, against Stengel's advice, continued to play with a heavy brace supporting the damaged limb.

It was gutsy of him to play in pain, but what the public saw was the bottom line—a .295 average with 21 home runs and 92 RBIs. Solid statistics, but not the numbers of a superstar. And as heir apparent to DiMaggio, who had started his career with a bang—averages of .323 (29 home runs), .346 (46 home runs), and .324 (32 home runs) during *his* first three seasons—Mantle appeared to be a pale carbon copy.

His World Series performance in '53 added to that impression, casting doubt over whether the Yankees could rely on him, as they had on DiMaggio and Ruth before him, to be front and center in the pinch. The '53 Series had seen Mantle hit a grand-slam home run in one game but in another strike out four times against Carl Erskine, who kept his fastball in tight to Mantle. Mantle would bat only .208 in the six game series, which the Yankees won. Mantle's performance prompted Cannon to observe: "The sky may be serene and beautiful but the slightest puff of wind seems to blow a blizzard across your [Mantle's] day. Either they're measuring your home runs or tabulating your strikeouts."

Yankee fans offered up more boos and catcalls. There were a number of reasons for the fans' disaffection, from The Mick's emotional outbursts to his refusal to give the traditional tip of the cap to them on home runs, even though Stengel would urge him to. Mantle insisted he ran out his home runs with his head down so as not to embarrass the pitcher he'd just abused. But from the bleachers, Mantle seemed like a petulant, spoiled child.

Nor was The Mick's 4-F status a public relations boon. Shortly after the '52 season, Mantle had undergone another

The Mick shows off the ball he hit out of Washington's Griffith Stadium.

examination by his draft board. And though military rules now disallowed osteomyelitis as a cause for exemption from military service, it turned out that the right knee Mantle had injured in the '51 Series now disqualified him.

As Jerry Coleman, who would miss most of the '52 and '53 seasons while serving in the military, recalled: "When I came back from Korea, I heard people in the stands yelling at him, calling him a 4-F coward, awful things. Mantle would have paid his way to go to Korea. And yet people shouted those things, things that went right to a man's masculinity. If they had said those things to me, I think I would have killed somebody. But he never said a word: Mickey never complains about anything. But it had to bother him, it had to make him wonder: What kind of people would say those things? I've often wondered if it affected the way he acts toward people outside baseball."

🔻 🔻 🔻

"I ought to punch you in the nose."

In those early years, and even later, Mantle was not comfortable in public. In the clubhouse, among his teammates, he mixed easily. He would kibitz other Yankees, tell corny jokes, sing his country songs, and mimic other players. Unlike DiMaggio, who maintained a certain reserve, Mantle was one of the boys, always ready for a good time. For there was always a friendly word, a welcoming gesture from The Mick. He relished the company of his baseball peers and was always in the thick of the clubhouse give-and-take, partaking of the never ending needling and pranks in his raucous, rowdy way. In contrast to DiMaggio, Mantle's style was one-for-all and all-for-one.

And in those years, the Yankees were a closely knit ball club.

"We were very protective of each other," recalled Gene Woodling. "Pros should never, never talk about another ballplayer. If a Jim Bouton type had written a book about his teammates in my day, he would have been in serious trouble. You just didn't do those things."

Recalled Yankee teammate Tony Kubek: "Mickey always said, 'On my tombstone I want one thing: I was a good teammate.'"

He was every bit of that. And as a consequence, his teammates not only were fond of him, they also were his biggest supporters when critics assailed him.

But when The Mick stepped out of the clubhouse and was confronted by fans, his impulse was to avoid them and, if that was impossible, to bolt from them. In the wrong mood—if the team had lost or he had failed to play up to his standards—he could be rude and mean-spirited to people outside of baseball, even to earnest grade-schoolers seeking his autograph.

Yet there were times Mantle would go out of his way to be kind. On one occasion Mantle had seen a story in the *New York Daily Mirror* that told of the murder of an honor student who had been a Mickey Mantle fan and had been looking forward to a trip to Yankee Stadium with his father so he could see The Mick in action. Mantle was touched by the story and asked a Yankee functionary if he would type out a letter of sympathy to the parents of the deceased boy that Mantle could sign.

It was not an isolated instance. Throughout his career there would be moments that stood in stark contrast to those other boorish incidents involving Mantle. Following the 1962 All-Star game, Mantle was riding in a taxi from Griffith Stadium, site of the contest, to the hotel where the players were lodged. In the cab with him were American League All-Stars Rich Rollins and Camilo Pascual.

"On the way," said Rollins, "we stopped for a light. A kid pulled up in a car near us, saw Mickey sitting in the front seat, and hollered to him to autograph some kind of trophy case. Mickey didn't say anything but he got out of the cab, crossed over the lanes to the car, and signed the thing. Then he had to run back because the light had changed, and the horns were blowing behind us."

With the newsmen who covered the team, Mantle displayed

that same unpredictability. When a writer with a notepad approached him after a game, there was no telling what version of Mickey Charles Mantle would be awaiting him. In his early years, Mantle's shyness made him a limited interview—he tended to give yes/no answers rather than full-blooded responses. Some of the scribes marked him for shy, others for a rube. Joe Trimble would write in 1953: "Mantle isn't the brightest individual in the world, but neither is he a dolt. He is quiet, rather shy and inarticulate."

In time Mantle would grow somewhat more comfortable among the press. But it would not alter his moody nature. When things were going well, he could be humorous and open with writers. Then again, for no particular reason he might prove to be contrary. At such times he would hide out in the trainer's room, which was off-limits to the press, or, if he chose to sit at his locker, shoot them the *malocchio* (evil eye), or make a face and belch, or bluntly tell them to fuck off, get away from me.

"Mickey could always let a reporter know that he had asked his last question," Whitey Ford would say.

As author David Halberstam would note: "His anger, his ability to look right through men he dealt with every day, men whose reporting had in general helped build the myth of Mantle as the greatest ballplayer of his era, could be shattering. Once when Maury Allen, the beat writer on the *Post*, was standing near the batting cage and Mantle was taking batting practice, Mantle turned to him and said, 'You piss me off just standing there.' That became something of a motto in the Allen household when one member of the Allen family was irritated with another."

Mantle once told the *New York Daily News* columnist Dick Young: "I ought to punch you in the nose." His remark came after Young had criticized the Yankees for hiding from the press in the trainer's room after a loss. Young called it "childish." Mantle took umbrage.

As Young wrote: "I offered to sit down and talk this whole thing over, or something clever like that, but he just turned me loose with a grunt of disgust and walked away. Well, we didn't have many lunches together after that, and one day I'm sitting in Toots Shor's and feeling pretty lousy because there's a newspaper strike.

"I look across the room, and there's Mantle at a table with Frank Scott, the ballplayers' agent. Our eyes crossed and I nodded and went back to poking at whatever was in my plate. Suddenly, I felt somebody slipping into the next chair.

"'Mickey says he's willing to do a magazine piece with you,' said Scott, 'and you can keep the money. He knows you have a lot of kids.'"

❧　❧　❧

"... they can't tell midnight from noon."

At that time, reporters did not look hard into the personal lives of the players. Stories from the early fifties tended to depict Mantle, whose son, Mickey, Jr., was born in April '53, as a family man, living quietly during the season with Merlyn and son in a rented house in New Jersey, and in the off-season in a home in Oklahoma he'd bought with his $7,000 '52 World Series share.

The truth was otherwise. In season or out, Mantle was no homebody. To paraphrase Merlyn, Mantle was a father and a husband in a small geographic corner of his mind. During the season, particularly but not exclusively when the team was on the road, Mantle was enjoying his celebrity. The Yankee organization became aware of Mantle's partying and his drinking to excess—aware enough and concerned enough, eventually, to have private detectives tailing Mantle and the teammates with whom he regularly socialized, Billy Martin and Whitey Ford, and reporting back to the team their social itinerary.

Wherever they went, Mantle and company rarely returned early, prompting Stengel to say: "I got these players who got the bad watches, that they can't tell midnight from noon."

It hadn't taken Mantle long to adapt to the bright lights, and the booze that made them even brighter. The drinking was part of the ballplaying ritual.

"Maybe you've got drugs now, and maybe steroids and stuff like that in sports now," said Tony Kubek. "But back then beer and booze was the choice, the poor choice, that a lotta people made. You sat in the clubhouse sometimes and some of the guys just preferred, till the crowd cleared the street, to drink all the beer that was there."

It was beer that was readily available after Yankee games. This was not a big surprise. One of the ball club's sponsors was Ballantine Beer. But there was more to it than that commercial affiliation. As Kubek indicated, the times were different then. And so were attitudes. Downing a brew in Mantle's ballplaying era was a manly way to cool out after a ball game. And slugging down a few beers with teammates was part of the macho ethos of being an athlete. Beer had as much to do with team esprit as being a way to satisfy thirst.

These days, athletes are much more conscious of their bodies as a commodity whose productivity can be prolonged by regular conditioning and sensible nutrition—ideas that have been embraced by the larger society. Back in the fifties, athletes hadn't heard the term "aerobic exercise" and didn't have the sophisticated weight-training regimens in season and during off-seasons that are practically de rigueur now. A lot of them drank, a lot of them smoked—in 1954 Mantle was among a number of ballplayers whose name and likeness would be used to promote Camel cigarettes; unimaginable today.

If Mantle abstained from tobacco, he gave himself wholeheartedly to the late hours and drinking that became The Three Amigos' routine. The Yankee front office regarded his carousing as detrimental to his performance and, moreover, as unbefitting a Yankee. The team's general manager, George Weiss, had a certain image in mind of what a Yankee should be, and it was 180 degrees from the freewheeling, pubcrawling sorts that Mantle, Ford, and Martin represented. When it became apparent that Mantle and friends were unlikely to behave in a civil manner, Weiss continued to have them followed.

He was never happy about the chronic boozing that Mantle, Martin, and Ford partook of and was especially outraged when The Mick and his two cronies played fast and loose with the bill for a party celebrating the team's fifth straight American League pennant, in 1953. When the pennant had been clinched, the Yankee organization held a victory dinner for the players at the Stadium Club. But many of the Yankees felt the need to extend the celebration into the night, some fourteen of them turning up at the Latin Quarter, a nightclub featuring statuesque chorus girls and uptempo music.

Well, when the bill arrived, as a lark the name of Yankee co-owner Dan Topping was signed for the $700 tab that Mantle, Ford, Martin, and several other players had incurred. It led to a wake-up call from an angry Weiss early the following morning, demanding that Martin and Mantle get to his office pronto.

When they arrived, he announced he was fining them $1,000, not for their chicanery the previous night at the Latin Quarter but rather for their season-long excesses. He then passed them on to Topping, who started off by threatening to turn them over to the authorities for forgery but ended up simply padding their fine by an additional $500 each.

As the Yankees' best player, Mantle had leeway that lesser talents would not have been afforded. While the Yankee front office did not condone his partying, and though Stengel warned him it couldn't possibly enhance his game, Mantle did as Mantle pleased. That is the way of sports. The top guns always are cut slack that the marginal players aren't.

But in Mantle's case, the drinking would not simply be a matter of boyish excess that time and maturity would moderate. The drinking would prove to be a crutch he increasingly relied on. What propelled it? Likely his shyness was a factor. Mantle was never entirely comfortable being the big-time star he was, and alcohol went a long way in making him less self-conscious.

Then there was the complex relationship with his father. While Mantle was a gifted athlete, a phenom, from early on he felt the pressure to succeed. Anything short of success would be an affront to Mutt, and the thought of disappointing his father weighed heavily on him. The wetting of his sheets was an early and vivid indication of the burden under which young Mickey toiled, and the pressure it exerted on him. That bed-wetting surely didn't fit the heroic image of Mantle that the public had of him. Indeed, years later, when Mantle mentioned the bed-wetting on a 1970 *Dick Cavett Show* on which songwriter/musician Paul Simon was also a guest, Simon was dumbstruck. "Mickey Mantle wet the bed?!"

Yet the tension at the heart of Mutt's quest did not go away when Mantle became a big-leaguer; nor did it disappear even when his father died. Years later, when drink had driven Mantle to enter the Betty Ford Center in December 1993, he remembered his preadmission interview:

"I told the counselor that I drank because of depression that came from feeling I'd never fulfilled my father's dreams. I had to write my father a letter and tell him how I felt about him. You talk about sad. It only took me ten minutes to write the letter, and I cried the whole time, but after it was over, I felt better. I said that I missed him, and I told him I loved him. I would have been better off if I could have told him that a long time ago. . . ."

To the Yankees' stiff-collared executives, particularly Weiss, the role of Billy Martin in Mantle's carousing was a source of discontent. Martin was viewed by the front office as a catalyst and provocateur in Mantle's drinking binges—in short, a bad influence on The Mick. And though Martin was a solid force in the Yankee lineup, as time went by, the front office disenchantment with his effect on Mantle would grow—and jeopardize his place on the team.

For Mantle, Martin was the street-sharp, outgoing companion he always seemed to be attracted to—the big-league version of Lou Skizas. As it happened, Skizas was still toiling in the minor leagues, hoping to get his chance to play in the majors. (Skizas finally would make it to the major leagues in 1956. His career lasted four seasons, 1956–1959, during which time he played for four different American League teams—New York, Kansas City, Detroit, and Chicago—and had a lifetime batting average of .270).

With Ford, the three Yankees kept late hours and enlivened the drinking establishments of American League cities. It was not unheard of for "The Three Amigos" to see the sun come up after a night of imbibing.

Indeed, stories abounded of Mantle's arriving at ballparks haggard after a night of boozing and sometimes without the benefit of sleep, and yet managing to summon the muscle memory to hit the baseball out of the park. But while that actually happened on several occasions, and Stengel and Yankee teammates may have marveled at his recuperative resources, the big picture that the team's front office had was that Mantle could be more productive than he was through those years, 1952–1955.

❦ ❦ ❦

"I could have made a difference."

While Mickey's statistics were sound—he had back-to-back .300 years in 1954 (.300) and 1955 (.306, with a league-leading 37 home runs)—there was a feeling among Yankee brass that The Mick could be even better if he put his mind to it. And if that were to happen—if Mantle could register Ted Williams–like statistics—well, then more glory would accrue to the Bronx Bombers. In short, the Yankees needed him to be the best Mickey Mantle he could possibly be.

Mantle's 37 home runs were, the Yankee brass liked to believe, still another proof of the potential he had. While Mantle had hit tape-measure home runs during his brief career, 1955 was the first year he had challenged the league's leaders in that category. A few of his 37 home runs he attributed to the perspicacity of Yankee pitcher Bob Turley. Studying the pitchers on other teams, Turley often was able to predict what they would throw from telltale habits of theirs.

For instance, Cleveland's Early Wynn positioned his glove differently according to what pitch he meant to deliver. Other pitchers left similar clues.

"One day on the bench, I was sitting next to Mantle," recalled Turley, "and showed him that I could predict all the pitches. He said, 'God almighty, let's work something out.' So during all my years in New York [1955–1962], Mickey and I would have all kinds of signs based on my whistling to let him know what was coming."

Had the Yankees continued to extend their World Series streak beyond the five straight they had won through 1953, the team's executives might have been less disposed to expect more from Mantle. But toward the mid-fifties, the Yankees slipped a bit from their standard of excellence. In 1954 the Yankees won 103 games, which in most years would have assured them the pennant. Not this time, though. The American League champion Cleveland Indians won 111 games and then were beaten in the World Series by the New York Giants and an improbable pinch-hitting hero named James Lamar (Dusty) Rhodes. Rhodes had crucial hits in the first three games as the Giants swept the Indians in four straight.

The next year, 1955, the Yankees won the American League pennant again, but they would not have the benefit of a 100 percent healthy Mantle when they went up against their interborough rival, the Brooklyn Dodgers. The Dodgers had never won a World Series. Since 1941, the Dodgers had been beaten in five trips to the Series by the Yankees. The regularity of those defeats had made the Dodgers baseball's longest-running soap opera. No matter how hard the Dodgers tried, they came up short at Series time. The frequency with which they lost—and the undying optimism of the Dodger rooters—had inspired a rallying cry of "Wait till next year!" Always next year.

For a team that was regarded as snakebitten, the Dodgers caught a break when Mantle's effectiveness was severely reduced by a pulled hamstring muscle incurred while running out a bunt late in the '55 season. In the seven-game Series, Mantle was able to appear in only three games, once as a pinch-hitter, and performed without great success. He managed a meager 2 hits in 10 at-bats.

Still, the Series came down to the seventh and final game, one that the injured Mantle would begin from the bench. What he saw was a strategic move by Dodger manager Walter Alston turn out to be crucial in the outcome of the game. In the sixth inning Alston brought Junior Gilliam in from leftfield to replace Don Zimmer at second base and put the lefthanded Sandy Amoros in Gilliam's spot.

An inning later, the Yankees threatened. Dodger pitcher Johnny Podres walked Billy Martin, then Gil McDougald bunted for a base hit. That brought Yankee catcher Yogi Berra to bat. Berra sliced a drive down the leftfield line. Amoros raced toward the ball at full speed. For a moment it appeared he had too much distance to cover. But Amoros kept coming. With the stands along the leftfield foul line looming before him, he reached out his glove. Had he been a righthanded fielder, he would have had to reach across his body. But as a lefthanded fielder, the glove was on his right hand, which allowed him to extend his arm fully. The ball landed in the webbing. Amoros dug his spikes into the turf, pivoted, and threw to shortstop Pee Wee Reese, who whirled and fired the ball to Gil Hodges at first. The retreating McDougald could not get back to first in time and was doubled up. The Yankee rally was snuffed. The Dodgers would go on to win the first World Series in their history.

Mantle would appear in that final game as an unsuccessful

pinch-hitter and later would rue his inability to play at full efficiency for the Series.

"Not to take anything away from the Dodgers, who had a great team, but I think if I had been healthy, I could have made a difference," he said.

Meanwhile, Yankee fans and front office executives waited for Mantle to deliver, finally, on a phenom's promise.

circa 1956

CHAPTER FIVE

EMERGENCE OF A SUPERSTAR

If the team that Mantle joined in '51 as a rookie was regarded as "DiMaggio's Yankees," by '56 the team had become "Mantle's Yankees."

While Stengel shuffled his lineups regularly, platooning players without a second thought, the switch-hitting Mantle was one of the few Yankees the manager kept in the lineup day in, day out. By now Mantle had become the soul of the team.

"There was verbal leadership coming from guys like Hank Bauer, who would remind everyone that they'd have to play hard to make the World Series," recalled Turley. "Then there was silent leadership from guys who would go out there and bust their asses every day. Mantle was a silent leader. He loved to play baseball and would do his best every day."

The team's personnel had changed as Mantle entered his sixth big-league season.

Joe Collins, who had started at first base in '51, was now a backup to the crew-cut, muscular Bill Skowron, known to his teammates as "Moose." Jerry Coleman, the second baseman in '51, played behind Billy Martin. Bobby Brown, who had started at third base, had retired after the '54 season to pursue a career in medicine. Andy Carey was the new third baseman. McDougald was the shortstop, and the rarely used Rizzuto was on the bench. In the outfield, DiMaggio had retired, Woodling had been traded, and Bauer, Mantle, and Howard were the outfield starters by '56. Berra remained the catcher.

The pitching aces from the '51 team—Raschi (21–10), Lopat (21–9), and Reynolds (17–8)—had all retired, and in their place New York would have to rely on Ford, Turley, Johnny Kucks, Tom Sturdivant, Bob Grim, Tommy Byrne, and one Donald James Larsen, who would make history that October.

But in the beginning, and through the end, '56 would be remembered for what Mickey Mantle wrought. For the first time in his career, the brilliance he had shown previously in bursts would shine through a full season, as Mantle justified every penny of the $32,500 salary he was paid.

The season would begin with a bang in Washington. After President Dwight David Eisenhower threw out the first ball on Opening Day, April 17, 1956, Mantle would light into a Camilo Pascual fastball in his first at-bat and send it soaring over the centerfield wall of Griffith Stadium, out of the ballpark, and onto the roof of a building on Fifth Street. Estimated distance? Four hundred sixty-five feet.

A fine beginning, certainly. Mantle would end up with another home run as the Yankees won on Opening Day, 10–4.

In the Yankees' first home game, against the Red Sox, Mantle had two hits, one of them a three-run home run, as Ford pitched the Bombers to a 7–1 victory. A day later, Stengel tried to dissuade him from playing with a pulled thigh muscle. But The Mick insisted he was OK, and then went out and got three hits—one of them a home run into the upper deck in right field—as the Yankees won, 14–10.

So it went. From Opening Day, Mantle at the bat was a fearsome sight to American League pitchers. Not only was he hitting the ball with power, he also was suddenly a hard out. No longer was he chasing bad pitches as he often he had in previous years. Mantle said that Stengel's decision to put Berra in the cleanup slot, right behind him in the batting order, worked to his advantage. Pitchers were now forced to get the ball in the strike zone for fear of walking him and then having to pitch to Berra, a dangerous hitter in his own right. Whatever. There was no question Mantle finally was producing like the superstar the Yankees had trumpeted from 1951.

Through April and his first 16 games, he was batting .433 with 11 home runs, provoking speculation in the press that here at last was a player who might be capable of breaking Babe Ruth's seasonal home run record of 60.

"A tree-mendous ballplayer," Stengel said. "Don't matter what ballpark he's in either. One of those shots Mantle hit in Washington might be traveling yet except it strikes a tree outside the park. They tell me that the only other feller which hit that tree was Ruth. He shook some kids outta the tree when the ball landed. But the tree's gotten bigger in twenty-five years, and so, I guess, have the kids the Babe shook outta it."

As April gave way to May, Mantle continued hammering the baseball with his 32-ounce bat when he hit lefthanded, 10 ounces lighter than Ruth's, or with a 36-ounce bat when he went to the plate righthanded. With nearly one-third of the season played, he was hitting .425 with 20 home runs and 50 RBIs. Of those home runs, the one that would make veteran baseball observers goggle-eyed was the shot he hit on Memorial Day at Yankee Stadium against Washington's Pedro Ramos. For with that blast Mantle came as close as any major-leaguer had to hitting a home run out of Yankee Stadium. The ball Mantle struck nearly went over the 117-foot-high gray-green facade of the roof in rightfield.

As Robert W. Creamer was to write in *Sports Illustrated*: " . . . in the 33 years since the stadium was opened not one of the great company of home run hitters who have batted there—the list includes Babe Ruth, Lou Gehrig, Joe DiMaggio, Jimmy Foxx, Hank Greenberg and about everyone else you can think of—had even come close to hitting a fair ball over the giant-sized filigree hanging from the lip of the stands which in both right and left field hook far into fair territory toward the bleachers. . . .

"The ball struck high on the facade, barely a foot or two below the edge of the roof. Ever since, as people come into the stadium and find their seats, almost invariably their eyes wander to The Spot. Arms point and people stare in admiration. . . ."

Suddenly, baseball men were speaking only in superlatives when it came to Mantle.

• Al Lopez, manager of the Cleveland Indians: "Mantle has more power than Babe Ruth."

• Bill Dickey, Yankee batting coach who had played with both Ruth and Lou Gehrig: "I thought when I was playing with Ruth and Gehrig, I was seeing all I was ever gonna see. But this kid . . . Ruth and Gehrig had power, but I've seen Mickey hit seven balls, seven, so far . . . and I've never seen nothing like it."

• Joe DiMaggio: "Mickey has grown up. It takes some players longer to arrive than others. He has learned to pick out the ball he wants to hit."

• Ted Williams: "Don't worry about Mantle. In another

fifteen or twenty years, you'll be voting for him for the Hall of Fame."

For Mantle, there was no higher tribute than to have Williams appraise him so flatteringly. To The Mick, the Red Sox's Splendid Splinter, as Williams was called, was the quintessential hitter in the game.

For New York fans, Mantle's great season in '56 came at a time when there were three major-league teams in New York— the Yankees, Dodgers, and Giants. It came at a time that would be seen, in retrospect, as a golden age of baseball.

It was not just that there were three big-league franchises in the city that made it such a thrilling era. No, there was more to it than that. Those ball clubs, as it happened, were a treasure trove of talent. And the New York fans were rabid in their appreciation of that talent.

With the folks in Brooklyn, there was the added dimension

New York's three great outfielders, Mantle, Dick Snider, and Willie Mays, together in 1981.

of Brooklyn's being a sort of poor relative to the more exalted borough of Manhattan. This caused them, as the team's broadcaster Red Barber was to note, to unite "behind the Dodgers as part answer to the tall, proud spires of Manhattan. . . ."

The passions incited by the interborough rivalry in the fifties—Giants versus Dodgers during regular-season play, or Yankees versus Dodgers or Giants during the World Series—were like nothing the sport has known since. It is unlikely that one city will ever again have three baseball franchises. When the Dodgers and Giants departed for the West Coast after the 1957 season, an era came to a crashing halt.

❖ ❖ ❖

"I never saw anything like it."

Ｂut in memory, the era lives. And for many, that wealth of talent that once dazzled a great city was defined by centerfield, which in Yankee Stadium meant Mantle, in Ebbets Field (where the Dodgers played) meant Duke Snider, and in the Polo Grounds (where the Giants toiled) meant Willie Mays.

For New York baseball aficionados, the debate of most intense passion would focus on which of the three centerfielders—Mays, Mantle, or Snider—was the best.

In '56 it was Mantle, hands down.

The Mick kept pounding the baseball through the summer, though not at the accelerated pace he'd had earlier in the year. Going into August, he had hit 34 home runs, and his chances of catching Ruth seemed unlikely. But in August, Mantle was smokin'. Pitchers of great repute and those whose names barely registered with the baseball public were abused by Mantle for home runs.

With his 13 home runs in August, Mantle went into the final month of the regular season with 47 home runs—and an outside chance at catching Ruth.

Mantle, not Mays, and not Snider, was the dominant centerfielder in '56 in all the boroughs and beyond. For Mantle's admirers, his feats on the diamond were enhanced by the fact that he played with a warrior's indifference to pain. Each day Yankee trainer Gus Mauch would massage Mantle's legs and then The Mick would tape himself, wrapping bandages from low on his right shin to the top of the thigh. Because the tape restricted circulation, Mantle would not take batting practice before a doubleheader, taping up just before the first game.

With his heroics, Mantle's public exposure—never slight to begin with—intensified. In July 1956 the *New York Daily Mirror* even ran a series, "My Life with Mickey!," that told of Mantle from Merlyn's point of view:

> Over in River Edge off Route 4 in Bergen County, New Jersey, Merlyn Mantle, a red-haired, green-eyed mid-Western girl of 24 is in shorts, lying on a chaise longue in the patio of a comfortable five-room ranch-type house. She has her own noisy crowd— Mickey Elvin Mantle, three years old and the image of his father, and David, six months old.
>
> . . . Mrs. Mantle is a housewife and mother, a girl who wistfully wishes she saw her husband more. For her, though she's the wife of the bright young star, there's little of the glamor. It's rather like being the wife of a travelling salesman.
>
> "After being married to Mickey for four years, I

feel I'm fairly well acquainted with him," she says. "But he's only home for about two weeks at a time during the season. And then he never gets home until 7:30. He tries to make it before I put the children to bed. And even when he's in New York, he has so many things to do during the day besides playing baseball. . . . We don't see each other very much."

The Yankees clinched the '56 pennant on September 18. On the same day, Mantle hit his fiftieth home run of the season, off Billy Pierce of the White Sox. Although his chances of catching Ruth were remote, The Mick was well ahead of Cleveland's Vic Wertz for the American League home run crown.

Mickey and Merlyn enjoying a night on the town at New York's Harwyn Club.

But as the season wound down, the pressure was on Mantle to lead the league in batting average and RBIs as well as home runs. The three categories were known as the Triple Crown. If he could win the Triple Crown, he would be the first player to accomplish it since his idol Ted Williams did it in 1947.

Ironically, it was Williams who was his greatest threat to being the league's leading hitter as the '56 season wound down. In the RBIs category Mantle was being closely pursued by Detroit's Al Kaline.

As fate would have it, the Yankees ended the regular season by playing a three-game series against the Red Sox in New York. That meant that Mantle and Williams would be within each other's gun sights as they went for the batting title. Going into the series, Mantle was batting .354 and Williams .350. The Mick had 127 RBIs while Kaline had 124. Mantle, who had sat out a few games with a muscle pull, was back in the lineup when Boston came to town.

As he said: "I didn't want to be sitting on the bench with the batting title at stake."

In the first game of the Yanks-Red Sox series, Mantle had 1 hit in 4 at-bats, his 52nd home run. (Wertz would finish a distant second in the American League, with 32 home runs.) Williams went hitless in 3 at-bats. Mantle's average was .353, Williams's .348. Mickey led Kaline in RBIs, 128 to 124.

Mantle did not start the next game against Boston. Instead, he was used as a pinch-hitter and drew a walk with the bases loaded. With Williams going 1 for 6, his average dropped to .345 while Mantle's average remained at .353. That left one more game of regular-season play.

As Mantle recalled: "Williams conceded the batting title. He didn't play the final game, finishing with a batting average of .345 at the age of thirty-eight, which is truly amazing. I didn't start either, but I pinch-hit for Jim Coates in the ninth inning and knocked in a run with a ground ball. I finished with a .353 average and the batting title.

"Now I had to sweat out word from Detroit to find out if I had won the Triple Crown. Kaline gave it his best shot. He knocked in two runs in the last game to finish with 128, two behind me. I had won the Triple Crown.

"I was only the twelfth Triple Crown winner in baseball. I also led the major leagues in home runs, RBIs, and batting average, only the fourth player to do that, and I was in pretty good company. Rogers Hornsby had done it for the St. Louis Cardinals in 1925. Lou Gehrig had done it for the Yankees in 1934. And my idol Ted Williams had done it for the Red Sox in 1942."

Proud as he was of his Triple Crown triumph, Mantle felt the season would be incomplete unless the Yankees could regain the world championship. Their World Series rival once again would be the Dodgers.

The Series was tied at two games apiece when Larsen went up against Brooklyn's Sal Maglie in Yankee Stadium on October 8, 1956.

Larsen's pitching style had changed during the year. Toward the end of the '56 season he had decided to simplify his pitching motion. He did this by giving up the elaborate windup he used before each toss. With no windup at all, he thought he could keep batters off balance and conceal the different grips he used for his assortment of pitches.

Larsen's no-windup style had baffled the Dodgers. One Dodger batter after another tried to reach base safely against Larsen and could not.

As Mantle recalled: "I was standing beside Larsen in the Yankee dugout when we were at bat in the seventh inning and

"The Splendid Splinter"—Boston's Ted Williams.

he said to me, 'Wouldn't it be something if I pitched two more innings with a no-hitter?'"

It is a baseball superstition that players do not mention that a pitcher has a no-hitter going until the end of a game, as if verbalizing it will tempt the Fates to generate a hit for the opposition.

"I walked away from him [Larsen]," Mantle recalled. "We

all got the same idea about that time and cleared away from Don. . . . Larsen wasn't nervous but all the rest of us were."

And finally it came down to the last out, New York leading, 2–0. The Dodgers sent Dale Mitchell up to pinch-hit for Maglie.

"I was nervous from the eighth inning on," Mantle said. "But Mitchell was an extra strain because he sprays hits all over and it is not easy to play him."

The count on Mitchell went to 1 ball, 2 strikes. The crowd hushed as Larsen stared at Berra for his signal. He gripped the ball and then let it fly. It was his 97th pitch of the day. Mitchell cocked his bat and decided the ball would miss the strike zone. He was wrong. Umpire Babe Pinelli called him out on strikes. Don Larsen had pitched a perfect game. Twenty-seven men up, twenty-seven men out.

The Yankees led the Series, three games to two. But the Dodgers came back in game six, winning 1–0 in ten innings. The next day for the deciding game of the Series, the Yankees had the answer. Or at least Berra did. In New York's first inning, Yogi started things with a two-run home run off Dodger pitcher Don Newcombe.

In the third he hit another two-run home run to give the Yankees a 4–0 lead.

Elston Howard and Bill Skowron also homered as the Yankees won, 9–0, to clinch the Series and make the bus ride home free of taunting.

Mantle had had 6 hits in 24 at-bats during the Series, with 3 home runs and 4 RBIs.

For Mantle, 1956 was his bust-out year, finally. The baseball writers voted him the American League's Most Valuable Player. Mantle was, as Merlyn would say, "the toast of New York."

"And I don't mean to be trite," she said. "There is nothing

THE SCIENCE OF HITTING

Though they formed a mutual admiration society, no two batters could have approached the act of hitting a baseball from as divergent philosophical outlooks as did Mickey Mantle and Ted Williams.

Williams, who played nineteen years in the major leagues and finished with a lifetime batting average of .344 (sixth best in baseball history), was a student of the game with an evolved philosophy about hitting.

Mantle's one idea on hitting was to swing like hell.

Williams was highly attentive to the strike zone, refusing to bite on pitches that did not suit him. As a result, when he retired from the game after the 1960 season, he had accumulated 2,019 walks in 7,706 at-bats. Only Babe Ruth drew more walks: 2,056 in 8,399 at-bats.

Where Mantle led the league five times in strikeouts (with a high of 126 in 1959), Williams struck out only 27 times in 1941 when he batted .406, the last batter to hit .400.

As an instinctive hitter, Mantle might admire Williams for his power and his bat control, but he couldn't really absorb all the nuances that went into the Red Sox slugger's thinking. Once, when Williams asked him which hand he used to grip the bat with and which hand to guide it, Mantle said, "How the hell do I know?"

Mantle remembered the time when Williams broke down the mechanics of hitting for him—lots of talk about arched elbows and planted feet and unlocked hips. As Mantle recalled, he got practically cross-eyed from listening to Williams's very technical analysis, and feared that if he took any of it to heart he would throw himself out of whack. Mantle was a believer in the K.I.S.S. approach: keep it simple, stupid. Swing like hell.

As the 1956 season came down to its final weeks, it would be Mantle and Williams who would be vying for the batting crown. When Williams was asked to assess his chances, he focused on the great natural speed that Mantle had, speed that translated to numerous infield base hits over the course of a season.

Williams, who was not fast, said: "If I could run like that son of a bitch, I'd hit .400 every year."

quite like it, the status, the attention, the power of being a New York icon. It really is true: If you can make it there, you can make it anywhere.

"It was fantasy time. We were having our babies, going to some really neat places, and, in my imagination, having breakfast at Tiffany's. I thought I had the perfect marriage. *Look at me*, I thought. *I'm married to Mickey Mantle.* Who wouldn't want to be married to Mickey Mantle . . . ?

❖   ❖   ❖

"It was fantasy time."

In truth, it would never be "easy" for Merlyn to have the normal home life for which she hoped, the kind of wholesome togetherness typical of the television sitcoms of the fifties. Hope though she might that The Mick would settle into fatherhood, she realized soon enough that he was never going to be Ward Cleaver, sitting in the easy chair with slippers and pipe and thoughtfully easing The Beaver through another childhood crisis. Mickey hadn't the stable character or the selflessness that make for a prize husband and father.

After the '56 season, the world was his to have. Mantle cashed in on his Triple Crown aura, hiring an agent, Frank Scott, who kept him busy that winter doing after-dinner speeches all over the country and endorsing various products, including a pancake mix called—what else?—"Batter Up." Through a friend, Harold Youngman, Mantle became a partner in the Mickey Mantle Holiday Inn in Joplin (MO), which would prove profitable. But when he invested $5,000 of his, against Merlyn's and Youngman's advice, to be a partner in a so-called insurance company, he discovered he'd been had by a con man the FBI was pursuing. Before the '57 season Mickey moved the family to Dallas, where he became involved in another business, a bowling alley that would fold within a few years.

As for The Mick's main business, when salary negotiations with the Yankees began for the '57 season, Mantle felt emboldened by his Triple Crown stats to ask for $65,000—double what he had earned in '56. New York general manager George Weiss blanched when he heard that number and argued that Mantle's asking price was way out of line. But Mantle insisted the price was right. Ted Williams, he knew, was earning $100,000, and Stan Musial and Willie Mays were making nearly the same as Williams. In response, Weiss threatened to reveal the private-eye reports he had accumulated over the past few years, which detailed Mantle's nightlife, and he even threatened to trade Mantle to Cleveland for Rocky Colavito and Herb Score. Mantle told Weiss he would give up baseball and run his businesses in Dallas.

In the end, Yankee co-owner Del Webb intervened, asking Mantle to report to spring training and promising him it would be worth his while. Webb was as good as his word. When Mantle turned up at camp in St. Petersburg, Florida, Webb agreed to pay him a salary of $65,000.

In St. Petersburg with his wife and two sons, Mantle was accorded star privileges. The family would stay in a house on the beach rather than the hotel at which most of the team lodged. Whereas Merlyn had done her own housework in the two-bedroom red-cedar shingle house in Commerce, in St. Petersburg, Mantle hired a maid to help. When the Mantles went out, it was in Mickey's brand-new Lincoln.

Still, for most of his Yankee career, Billy Martin and Whitey Ford were Mantle's most important friends. Often they were like frisky schoolboys, indulging in water pistol fights and outrageous pranks. But it was the booze that bonded them. Even in the off-season, Martin would show up in Oklahoma, and the two of them would sit in roadhouses and saloons getting potted. Mantle's drinking became so inimical to Merlyn that for a time she took her sons and left Mantle.

It didn't change the good-times relationship that The Mick and Martin had. But in '57, as the Yanks battled for another American League pennant, Martin's influence on Mantle would come under deep scrutiny by New York's front office, precipitated by what became known as The Copa Incident.

The night of May 15 was planned as a celebration of Billy Martin's twenty-ninth birthday. A group of Yankee players—Bauer, Berra, Mantle, Johnny Kucks, and a few of their wives—had dinner with Martin at Danny's Hideaway, a Manhattan restaurant. Afterward, the players decided to head over to The Copacabana, a nightclub, to see the entertainer Sammy Davis, Jr.

At an adjoining table was a group of men who belonged to a bowling team. Many of the bowlers had been drinking, and soon were directing crude and insulting remarks to the Yankee table. One thing led to another. Pretty soon Bauer, Martin, and Mantle had moved from the showroom to a private corner to talk things over with some of the bowlers.

There are different versions of what happened next.

One of the bowlers claimed Bauer knocked him cold, an allegation that Bauer would deny.

Mantle claimed the Copa's bouncers grabbed the ringleader of the bowlers' group and hit him with saps.

"This guy was lying under a chair and he was all busted up," said Mantle. "It looked like Roy Rogers had come rolling through there on his horse Trigger, and Trigger had kicked this guy in the face.

"The bouncer at the Copa hustled us out of the place and through the kitchen and out onto the street, where we got cabs out of there. The bouncer was trying to protect us."

The next day's newspapers called it this way: YANKEES BRAWL AT THE COPA. It was front-page news and to the image-minded Yankee brass practically a capital offense.

For years, Weiss had been wanting to ship Martin to another team, viewing him as a corruptive influence on Mantle. But Billy was a favorite of Stengel's, and that was enough to keep him in the fold. But with The Copa Incident, Martin became the designated scapegoat, particularly since a talented newcomer at second base, Bobby Richardson, made Martin expendable. Even though a judge dismissed the case for insufficient evidence, Martin was guilty of being on Weiss's enemies list.

On June 15 Weiss traded Martin, Ralph Terry, Woody Held, and Bob Martyn to Kansas City for Ryne Duren, Jim Pisoni, Milt Graff, and Harry Simpson.

Billy Martin was gone, and for Mantle it was sad news. But the banishment to Kansas City of his friend did not deter Mantle or the Yankees. Mantle had another banner year in '57: He batted .365 with 34 home runs and 94 RBIs.

➤ ➤ ➤

"It didn't look very good...."

Still, the baseball writers regarded Mantle's 1957 season as worthy of another Most Valuable Player award. But this time there was a controversy about Mantle's selection. Many felt that the writers unjustifiably slighted Ted Williams, who finished behind Mantle and Roy Sievers of Washington in the voting. Williams had led the American League in batting with a .388 average (38 home runs and 87 RBIs), a remarkable achievement for any man but practically a mythic feat for the thirty-nine-year-old player that Williams was.

Whether it was the alignment of the planets or the Yankees' loss to the Milwaukee Braves in the '57 World Series that prompted George Weiss to figure the league's Most Valuable Player ought to take a salary cut, who can say? But when Mantle received his contract for 1958, it was calling for him to take $10,000 less in salary. Weiss's rationale was that Mantle hadn't had as good a year as his Triple Crown season.

Once again, Yankee ownership intervened—this time Dan Topping as well as Del Webb—and Mantle ended up with $75,000, a $10,000 raise.

Weiss's impecunious style was typical of baseball executives back then. A plantation mentality existed, with front-office types such as Weiss treating players with contempt. Free agency and multimillion-dollar players' salaries were a long way off. For now, even players as stellar as Mantle had to coexist with a system that was often demeaning to them, a system that would not change until the St. Louis Cardinals' star centerfielder—three-time All-Star and seven-time Gold Glove winner Curt Flood—shook things up in 1969.

With the 1957 season over, the Dodgers announced they were leaving Brooklyn for Los Angeles, and the Giants abandoned New York for San Francisco. It was the first clue that the national pastime was undergoing an attitude adjustment. Where once red-blooded Americans liked to think of baseball as merely a game, with the move westward baseball was becoming a hard-core business. For now the owners were cashing in. In time, the unionized players would demand—and would get—a bigger piece of the action. And as the game begat lockouts and strikes and mercenary ballplayers, more than a few fans would say the hell with baseball.

Not everybody back in '57 loved the Yankees, or Mantle. Even though he had won successive MVP awards, it did not appear to satisfy the public. In some quarters Mantle was still seen as a disagreeable sort, a perception that owed to his temper tantrums when things were not going well. The Mick was still prone to kick water coolers and fling his batting helmet. Add to that his brusqueness with fans off the field and a decline from his MVP years—.304 (a league-leading 42 home runs, 97 RBIs) in '58, .285 (31 home runs, 75 RBIs) in '59, and .275 (a league-leading 40 home runs, 94 RBIs) in '60— and it fueled the long-simmering conviction that Mantle was not the real McCoy the way Ruth and DiMaggio had been.

By spring training 1960, following a shocking third-place Yankee finish and a 79–75 record in '59, Leonard Shecter of the *New York Post* wrote a series on Mantle titled "Problem Child," in which he had anonymous sources giving Freudian reasons for The Mick's behavior. ("It's a form of masochism. I think he wants the fans to boo him. It's like having his father in the stands.")

Shecter claimed that off the record there were Yankee players who quibbled with Mantle's methods. As he would write:

> Boiled down, consolidated, they go like this: Mantle isn't self-disciplined enough. He's inclined to do things the easy way. And there's no one willing to stand over him and make him do the things he should do.
>
> He doesn't train properly and there's nobody who'll tell him "you go out there and run 15 laps . . ." The price he pays for this is hard to measure, but

everybody is sure it's bigger than Mantle will be willing to pay when the time comes.

Another writer, Milton Gross, would note: "It is a simple fact of baseball life that when the super-star comes along, the management usually is awed into inaction. . . . Undoubtedly this is a hangover from the days of Babe Ruth, the first authentic super-star. Ruth came and went as he pleased, with a law unto himself and the most successful freelance operator in the history of the game, off the field as well as on it. To this day, Mantle trains himself, runs when he wants to, hits when he wants to and, according to rumor, is exempt from the disciplinary rules which apply to other members of the Yankees."

Even without Billy Martin, Mantle continued to be a hard-drinking man, still dogged by Weiss's private detectives. For Mantle, their constant surveillance got to be a joke. There were times when Mantle would have a cabdriver go around and around in circles just to monkey with the gumshoes who were keeping tabs on him. On another occasion, when The Mick "made" two men as private detectives, he and Ford joined them at their table, and a good time was had by all.

"Our life was a constant round of parties, meetings with celebrities, public attention," Mantle said.

As ever, Martle partied to the detriment of Merlyn and the family. In '57 the Mantles moved to Dallas, where Merlyn and her sons would stay yearround. Merlyn apparently had grown tired of coming east during the season to be near a husband and father who, in season or out, was rarely there for the family. Indeed, when his third son, Billy Giles Mantle, was born in November 1958, Mantle was off hunting with Billy Martin and his businessman friend Harold Youngman. Merlyn wept over his absence.

THE FLOOD CASE

In 1969, when the Cardinals traded Tim McCarver and Curt Flood to Philadelphia in a seven-player deal, Flood, who had hit over .300 six times and been a key member of Cardinal championship teams in 1964 and 1967, refused to report to the Phillies.

At the time, baseball players were tied to their teams by the reserve clause—rules that prohibited players from choosing which teams they wished to play for.

In effect, it made the player the lifetime property of the ball club, and in so doing obviously limited his bargaining power with that ball club. For most players, a contract was offered on a take-it-or-leave-it basis. If a player could not come to terms with his team, his only option was the suicidal one of refusing to play. No play, no pay.

If Mantle, as a superstar, had a bit more leverage than the average player in getting his money's worth, he was still boxed in by the reserve clause, which did not allow him to test his value in a free market. Flood's refusal to go to Philadelphia would trigger a series of events that would change the status quo that favored the owners.

Flood, who had begun his big-league career in 1956, felt that as a veteran player he ought to have a say in his future. The unilateral privileges of the team that owned him made him, he said, feel like a head of cattle. When Flood asked then commissioner Bowie Kuhn to declare him a free agent and was turned down, he filed a lawsuit against baseball that charged the game with antitrust violations. He also sat out the 1970 season to punctuate his argument that the system needed to be changed.

Eventually, in 1972, the U.S. Supreme Court ruled against Flood. But as Flood would say, "All the groundwork was laid for the people who came after me."

In 1975 an arbitrator granted free agency to players Andy Messersmith and Dave McNally, which had the effect of killing the reserve-clause system and clearing the way for today's free-agent system by which players' salaries soared.

All that thanks to Curt Flood.

Among his teammates Mantle was still just one of the boys, a leader on the field and a prime instigator in their search for low-brow amusements. Among those diversions, as teammate Jim Bouton would later reveal, was the Yankees' predilection for "beaver shooting"—a catchphrase for all variety of spying on women—from dugouts, through knotholes, from fire escapes. The prime objective of a beaver shoot was to see a woman naked or in *flagrante delicto*. Later, as the author of the book *Ball Four*, Bouton described a beaver-shooting expedition that occurred on the roof of the Shoreham Hotel in Washington, a prime location because the L-shaped wings of the hotel made the windows particularly vulnerable.

> The Yankees would go up there in squads of fifteen or so, often led by Mickey Mantle himself. You needed a lot of guys to do the spotting. Then someone would whistle from two or three wings away, "Pssst! Hey! Beaver shot. Section D. Five o'clock." And there'd be a mad scramble of guys climbing over skylights, tripping over each other and trying not to fall off the roof. One of the first big thrills I had with the Yankees was joining about half the club on the roof of the Shoreham at two-thirty in the morning. I remember saying to myself, "So this is the big leagues."

During the '58 World Series against the Milwaukee Braves and with the Yankees down three games to one, Mantle showed up in the clubhouse with a trick arrow—the kind that appears as though it's going in one ear and out the other. When teammates noticed him, Mantle announced the team was in a tough bind, then made a cross-eyed face. That may not have been why

Mantle always swung hard, with exciting results both good and bad.

the Yankees rallied to win the next three games of the Series and become world champions again, but it didn't hurt.

What's more, his teammates were aware of the increasing pain with which Mantle was forced to play. No longer was it just the knees that troubled him, as if that was not bothersome enough. In the '57 World Series, The Mick had damaged his right shoulder in a collision at second base with Milwaukee's Red Schoendienst. The shoulder was a problem now when Mantle batted lefthanded and swung hard. Worse, it pained him when he lifted the arm to a certain height, and forced him to make adjustments in his stance. Yet Mantle played on, in pain and without complaint.

By 1960, Mantle was in his tenth season with the Yankees. Of those who had been prominent on the '51 Yankees, besides Mantle only Berra and McDougald remained, and both of them were now reduced to being part-timers in Stengel's system of platooning. Berra shared catching duties with Elston Howard; McDougald filled in at third base for Clete Boyer and at second base for Richardson. Skowron was the first baseman, and Kubek was the shortstop. The outfield was Mantle, Hector Lopez, and Roger Maris, who had been traded to the Yankees from Kansas City with Joe DeMaestri and Kent Hadley for Bauer, Larsen, Norm Siebern, and Marv Throneberry.

In '51 Ford had been in the military, following a brilliant 9–1 rookie year. He was still one of the Yankees' pitching aces in '60, along with Ditmar, Turley, Ralph Terry (reacquired in a trade), Jim Coates, and relievers Ryne Duren and Luis Arroyo.

And Stengel was still the field manager, although his effectiveness was seen as diminishing.

"He was sixty-nine, getting a bit crotchety," recalled Mantle. "If he'd been up drinking all night he'd let his coaches run the team while he took a quick snooze on the bench, snoring and farting, and everybody would have to move."

As he went into the 1960 season, Stengel was reported to be receiving an $80,000 base contract, with elaborate pension payments and bonus clauses.

But it was not the money that kept Stengel on the job. In fact, he was a wealthy man from his investments in oil wells and his position as director of the Glendale (Calif.) National Bank. His wife, the former Edna Lawson, was a woman of means, too. Her father had made his fortune in real estate and willed his estate to her.

The Yankees' third-place showing in '59 had left Stengel in shaky possession of his managerial job. It was tacitly understood that another also-ran finish by the Bombers would finish Stengel's managerial regime.

At age sixty-nine, he was the game's second-oldest manager in major-league history. Only Connie Mack, who managed the Philadelphia Athletics until he was eighty-eight, was older, and Mack had this advantage: He was his own boss, the majority stockholder of the team.

Mantle's '59 performance—that .285 batting average with 31 home runs and 75 RBIs—had given the cold-blooded Weiss the ammunition he needed to get back at Mantle for the years in which Topping and Webb had overruled him. He insisted Mantle would need to take a $17,000 pay cut. Mantle fought it and agreed, finally, to taking $10,000 less in salary, which gave him $62,000 for 1960.

Mantle was not happy about the salary reduction, and it seemed to affect his performance. He struggled at the bat early in the year, and sometimes he lacked the alertness and hustle expected of a major-leaguer. When he mistakenly believed there were two outs and failed to run out a grounder against the Senators, figuring Maris would be an easy force-out at second base, the Yankee Stadium crowd booed when The Mick's mental lapse resulted in an easy double play.

For violating a cardinal rule of baseball—run out everything—Stengel immediately benched Mantle and replaced him with Bob Cerv. But Mantle bounced back the next night in Baltimore, turning the jeers of the crowd to cheers by hitting two home runs, including a game-winning shot off knuckleballer Hoyt Wilhelm.

Mantle and the Yankees would rebound from the calamitous '59 season and win the American League pennant by eight games over the Baltimore Orioles in 1960. Against the Pirates in the World Series, it looked like business as usual. For in the seventh game, the Yankees led, 7–4, going into the eighth inning, and New York's reliever, Bobby Shantz, had pitched

⬥ STENGEL ⬥

"THE OLE PERFESSOR"—
CASEY STENGEL

local cabdriver who had run down Stengel and broken his leg.

Yet Stengel, who became known as "The Ole Perfessor," would end up as the man who guided the Yankees to ten pennants and seven world championships in his twelve seasons with the Yankees—a record that surely quashed the notion that he couldn't run a baseball team.

Born on July 30, 1890, Stengel didn't start out to be in baseball. He was studying to be a dentist at Western Dental College in his hometown of Kansas City, Missouri, when he decided to give it up to pursue his real love, baseball.

Casey would enjoy a big-league career of fourteen seasons, during which he played outfield with the Dodgers, Pirates, Phillies, Giants, and Braves and had a lifetime batting average of .284. In his three World Series appearances he did even better, batting .393.

Stengel's reputation as a colorful character dated back to his playing days. The often-told story that gave credence to his daft image was of the

In earlier stints as a manager, at Brooklyn (1934–1936) and with the Boston Bees (1938–1940), and Boston Braves (1940–1943), Charles Dillon (Casey) Stengel had never had a first-division team.

Stengel's reputation was that of a loser.

In fact, one year while Stengel was managing the Braves he was thought so little of that a Boston sportswriter nominated as the man who had done most for the city a day Stengel came to bat, doffed his cap, and a sparrow flew out.

As Yankee manager, he had a semi-intelligible way of speaking that the press referred to lovingly as "Stengelese." But while the garrulous manager's doubletalk might have endeared him to the press and given the reading public the picture of a lovable clown at the helm, Stengel was no pushover.

As Mark Gallagher, author of *The Yankee Encyclopedia*, would write: "Make no mistake about this fact: Casey only spoke Stengelese when he wanted to and usually only to the press. His players understood Casey perfectly. . . . The funny image of Casey portrayed by an adoring press was often a facade. True, he was basically a warmhearted, kindly and humorous man, but there were other sides to Casey. He could be mean and intimidating and by 1960 he had abused the sensitivities of many players, especially the younger ones. . . . But in his own eyes, Stengel was critical of his players in an effort to promote individual improvement, and he attacked only those he felt talented enough to improve. Yet, his targets did

not take kindly to what was perceived as abuse."

With Mantle, Stengel was keen-eyed enough to recognize that The Mick would fare better in the outfield than at shortstop. While Stengel did not coddle Mantle, The Mick regarded him as a second father, particularly after Mutt died in 1952.

"He had the players, sure," said Mantle of the talent pool Stengel drew upon, "but he knew how to use them."

In 1966 Stengel was voted into the Baseball Hall of Fame in Cooperstown, New York.

five scoreless innings. If there were ever a time to unpack the crates of champagne with which the Yankees could celebrate as world champions, it was now. Or so it seemed.

Pittsburgh, however, refused to roll over. Pirate pinch-hitter Gino Cimoli started the eighth inning with a single. Then came a play that may have turned the game around. Pittsburgh's Bill Virdon rapped a grounder to Yankee shortstop Kubek—an easy double-play ball. But as Kubek crouched to field the ball, it took a bad hop—apparently after striking a pebble—and hit him in the throat. Kubek went sprawling to the dirt and was removed from the game. Instead of two outs with the bases empty, there were two Pirates on and no outs.

Pirate shortstop Dick Groat singled in a run to cut the Yankee lead to 7–5. Stengel removed Shantz and replaced him with Jim Coates—one of several decisions that would be questioned later. There were those who believed Stengel should have gone with the fireballing reliever Ryne Duren. Whatever. The Pirates took advantage. After Bob Skinner sacrificed, Roberto Clemente hit a chopper to Skowron. When Coates failed to cover first base, Clemente was safe, another run scored, and the Yankee lead was reduced to 7–6.

Stengel's decision to stick with Coates would raise eyebrows. Mantle was among those who questioned the manager's call, feeling that Coates was too rattled to perform effectively. When Coates tried to throw a fastball by Pirate reserve catcher Hal Smith, Smith hit it into the leftfield seats to give Pittsburgh a 9–7 lead going into the ninth inning.

But the Yankees were the class team of this era, and in the ninth inning they showed why. They scored twice, to tie the game at 9–9. In came Yankee pitcher Ralph Terry to hold the Pirates in check.

The first Pittsburgh batter he faced was the crew-cut second baseman Bill Mazeroski. Terry threw two pitches. The first one was a ball. The next was a fast slider, letter-high. Mazeroski swung and sent the ball soaring to the left-centerfield wall. At 3:36 P.M. on October 13, 1960, the ball cleared the wall and gave the Pirates the world championship.

Mantle cried afterward.

Two days later, Stengel was fired. The era of the Ole Perfessor was over.

circa 1959

CHAPTER SIX

THE LAST GOOD YEARS

The new Yankee manager was Ralph Houk, who'd been a rarely used reserve catcher with New York from 1947 to 1954 and then a Yankee coach and a sometime manager in the team's farm system.

While manageing the Yank's Denver ballclub in the mid-fifites, Houk had worked with future Yankee stars such as Richardson, Kubek, Tery Duren, amd John Blanchard.

When he took over the Yankees in '61, Houk ditched Stengel's system of platooning players and installed a more regular pitching rotation. He also tended to praise his players rather than criticize them, as Stengel had, creating an upbeat work atmosphere.

After he left baseball, Mantle would look back on his career and rate the '61 Yankees as the best New York squad he had ever played on. The infield was Skowron (first base),

Richardson (second base), Kubek (shortstop), and Clete Boyer (third base). The outfield had Berra in left, Mantle in center, and Maris in right. Howard was the catcher. Ford headed a pitching staff that included Bill Stafford, rookie Rollie Sheldon, Terry, Coates, and reliever Arroyo.

Among Yankee aficionados, the debate goes on—whether the '61 Yankees were superior to that '27 team for which Ruth and Gehrig played. The '27 Yankees featured five .300 hitters—Gehrig (.373), Ruth (.356), Earl Combs (.356), Bob Meusel (.337), and Tony Lazzeri (.309), and a deep pitching staff led by Waite Hoyt (22–7) and including 19-game winners Wilcy Moore and Herb Pennock and 18-game winner Urban Shocker. But where the power on the '27 Yankees was pretty much limited to Ruth and Gehrig, the Yanks had additional long-ball threats in Skowron, Berra, Blanchard, and Howard.

In '61 Mantle and Maris would hit home runs with such startling regularity that their heroics soon dominated the baseball news. The competitive New York press was quickly augmented by writers from all over the nation as well as from abroad, all of them charting the assault on The Bambino's record 60. Through 92 games Mantle had hit 37 home runs and Maris 36. In 1927 Ruth did not swat his 37th home run until his 114th game.

Over the years, Ruth's record had acquired a sanctity that saw potential record-breakers confronted by pitchers who refused to facilitate the batter's quest for 60. As a hitter closed in on Ruth's mark, pitchers tended to bait him with balls thrown out of the strike zone or, worse, at the batter's head. Ralph Kiner once observed that it was impossible to break Ruth's record while on your back.

But the fact that Maris and Mantle coexisted in the same batting order—Maris batting third, Mantle fourth—made it more dangerous for pitchers to walk them.

As the nation followed the Mantle-Maris home run rivalry, in late July the commissioner of baseball, Ford Frick, decreed that because the American League schedule now ran to 162 games, Ruth's record would have to be broken within 154 games to be considered official. Frick was widely criticized for his ruling.

Meanwhile, Mantle and Maris went about their business, hitting home runs and then trying to cope with the unrelenting postgame interviews. Soon enough it was a media circus, with reporters repeating the same questions over and over again, and newspaper headlines focusing on "The M & M Boys," as Mantle and Maris were sometimes called. Their Yankee teammates were often overlooked in the hullabaloo about the pair, but they did not seem to mind the attention paid to the sluggers. In the clubhouse they would kibitz the celebrated home run hitters when either of them wandered in.

As Mantle recalled: "All the guys—Yogi, Whitey, everybody—they'd take the pressure off of us. We'd come into the clubhouse and someone [would ask] . . . 'Hey, what did the M & M boys do yesterday?' Instead of, like, holding back and being quiet about it. They brought it right out in the open. They was kidding us all the time."

But the objects of the protracted attention would come to find it tedious and sometimes annoying, as when a newsman asked Maris how a .260 hitter could possibly be challenging Ruth. Maris stared at the man and then wondered aloud whether he was a reporter or an idiot.

On and on it went.

When Maris began clouting home runs at a record pace, staying neck and neck with Mantle, the experts predicted that Maris, not Mantle, would succumb to the pressure. The thinking was that Mantle was the real McCoy as a power hitter, and

ROGER MARIS:
THE RELUCTANT HERO

Shanley High School in Fargo, North Dakota, did not have a baseball team, but that did not stop Roger Maris from being recognized as a superior athlete.

Maris excelled at basketball and at track, and was an all-state fullback in football. During summers he played baseball in midget leagues and, as he got older, in American Legion competition.

When he graduated from Shanley High, Maris bypassed a football scholarship offer to the University of Oklahoma and signed with the Cleveland Indians for a $15,000 bonus.

Where Mantle was regarded as a potential superstar before he had even played a major-league game, Maris had to persuade major-league managers that he was good enough to be a full-time player. In his first three seasons, at Cleveland and at Kansas City, he batted .235 (14 home runs, 51 RBIs), .240 (28 home runs, 80 RBIs), and .273 (16 home runs, 72 RBIs)—the stats of an average player.

But when he was traded to the Yankees in 1960, Maris sparked up. He batted .283 with 39 home runs and a league-leading 112 RBIs, and was voted the Most Valuable Player in the American League.

Before his historic 1961 season, Maris had never given any indication that he had the power to make a run at Babe Ruth's record. Sixty home runs? Maris never had hit even 40. To Yankee fans and to the baseball press, the idea of a Roger Maris as Ruth's successor struck a discordant note.

The irrational distaste for Maris—

and the pack journalism that tracked his season—eventually got to the player. A modest, straightforward individual, Maris came to despise the sideshow that accompanied the home run battle of The M & M Boys. The foolish questions. The false rumors of enmity between Mantle and him. The tediousness of it all. Maris was unnerved. Toward the end of the season, as he and Mantle became the first players on the same team ever to hit 50 home runs in the same season, Maris's hair began falling out as a result of the media pressure.

In retrospect, it is ironic that Maris's home run production tailed off dramatically after the '61 season.

He hit 33 home runs for the Yankees the following season, 1962, but never more than 26 in the years that followed. In a career that started in 1957 and ended in 1968, Maris's 1961 home run explosion would have an almost freakish quality.

But as it was happening, it was Topic A of the sports world. Would The Mick or Maris break the great Ruth's record?

By now, he and Mantle had grown close enough in the quest for 60 to be sharing a 3 1/2-room apartment in the Richmond Hill section of Queens with another teammate, Bob Cerv.

Ahead lay the stretch run.

MARIS HITS NUMBER 61.

Maris was a mere pretender. The Mick was suddenly the darling of the bleacherites, and Maris had replaced him as their public enemy.

As Robert Lipsyte would write: "Maris was not 'Ruthian,' sportswriters were intoning, it would be a shame if he broke the sacred mark. His every move was interpreted through the prism of his 'unworthiness.'

"It had always been Mantle who brushed off autograph-seekers, who turned his back on reporters, while Maris stood and signed, or sat and thoughtfully answered questions until the last microphone and notebook were gone.

"But it was Mantle who now got the good ink while Maris got 'ripped.'"

What that meant as the media onslaught intensified late that season was that Mantle—spotlighted from the git-go as a nineteen-year-old phenom—had become used to dealing with the press while Maris had not. Nothing in the baseball odyssey of Roger Eugene Maris could have prepared him for the summer of '61.

When he hit his 50th home run, Roger Maris got goose bumps.

"It got to be routine after that," recalled teammate Bob Cerv. "Every time Roger hit one into the seats, he'd break out in goose bumps."

With 18 games remaining on the regular-season schedule, Mantle had 53 home runs and Maris had 56.

At that point, The Mick caught a head cold . . . and a bad break. The bad break turned out to be a worse. The story goes like this:

When team broadcaster Mel Allen saw that Mantle was not feeling well, he suggested that The Mick go to a doctor of his whose clientele included several celebrities. The doctor gave

Mantle a shot, plunging the needle into his buttocks but up too high as far as Mantle was concerned. He screamed in pain and later would recall: "It felt as though he had stuck a red-hot poker in me."

Mantle said he felt momentarily paralyzed and so woozy that by the time he hit the street an elderly woman passing by asked him if he needed help. Mantle leaned against a building and asked her if she would call him a taxicab.

The shot left him so feverish the next morning that Mantle had to phone Houk and tell him he would be unable to play that night.

From his encounter with the doctor's needle, Mantle developed an abscess on his hip that had to be lanced so it could drain. But he was still in bad shape, no longer from the head cold but from the so-called remedy for it—the doctor's injection. What's more, he now had a surgical wound that was almost four inches by two—so wide and so deep that it could not be stitched over.

Mantle started only two more games after that, hitting his 54th home run in Boston. But he was not really recovered from his encounter with that hypodermic needle, and would miss 16 of the last 18 regular-season games. As Cerv recalled: "When Roger was gunning for home runs 60 and 61, Mickey was in New York's Lenox Hill Hospital, recuperating from an abscess infection."

Maris hit his 61st home run off Red Sox pitcher Tracy Stallard in the last game of the season, at Yankee Stadium. The ball landed in the lower deck of the rightfield stands, to the right of the bullpen and about six rows back.

For Mantle, Maris, and the Yankees, it was a remarkable season. The Yankees won the American League pennant by eight games over Detroit, and flexed their muscles while doing so. The team pounded out 240 home runs—more than any team in either league . . . and by a lot. Next best in the American League had been Los Angeles, with 189 home runs. In the National League, Milwaukee had the most home runs, with 188.

❖ ❖ ❖

"I could do no wrong."

The 240 home runs were also a major-league record. Maris (61), Mantle (54), Skowron (28), Berra (22), Howard (21), and Blanchard (21) constituted the most potent phalanx of sluggers in baseball history. By comparison, in 1927, when the Ruth-Gehrig Yankees won the pennant, the Bronx Bombers had led the majors with 158 home runs.

Mantle finished the season batting .317 in 153 games, with those 54 home runs and 128 RBIs. For Mantle, the '61 season was just as important for redefining public perception of him. Maris was the catalyst in Mantle's suddenly finding favor with fans everywhere. In '61, as the public withheld its acclamation for Maris and even turned antagonistic, throwing nuts and bolts and half-filled bottles at him from the stands, it embraced The Mick. From '61 on, he was beloved in New York and far beyond. Never more would he be viewed as the pale shadow of Ruth and DiMaggio.

Maris had given him that. The fickle fates that decide a man's public standing had gone against Maris, 61 home runs notwithstanding. For whatever reasons, the fans were resistant to this very decent, unpretentious man.

"After Roger beat me in the home run race in 1961," said Mantle, "I could do no wrong. Everywhere I went I got standing ovations. All I had to do was walk out on the field. Hey, what the hell? It's a lot better then having them boo you. . . . I became the underdog, they hated him and liked me."

The change in his reception seemed to mellow Mantle. Sportswriter Bert Sugar said the Mantle he encountered after '61 was "a nicer person."

"Particularly at a bar," said Sugar, "where he liked his scotch. Mickey had no pretense. He wasn't hung up on being Mickey Mantle. I'd run into him in places like Mr. Laff's, Runyan's, Tucker's—bars where sports guys hung out. And he'd always say, 'Hey, why don't you come over and say hello?' In a bar, Mickey was quiet—he wasn't a noise-r. He was very

Mantle signing a new contract for the 1962 season.

comfortable being in a crowd. He was happy being accepted as a person rather than Mickey Mantle.

"We'd tell one another jokes. He loved jokes, the longer the better. He didn't like one-liners. He went for good ole boy humor—I'm framing this, pre-1990s—you know, politically incorrect women jokes were the brunt of it. Mickey Mantle was a frat boy at heart."

The perpetual frat boy was a hit in the Yankee clubhouse. On the home front, though, he continued to be less than an exemplary husband and father to his sons, including his fourth son, Danny, born in March 1960. Mantle remained blithely unaware of their progress through Lamplighter's School in Dallas and seldom inquired about the particulars of their development. If his son Billy had dyslexia, it fell to Merlyn to see that he got help. In a way Mantle was more like a favored uncle to his sons, appearing from time to time and handing out money while advising them that it was time to see the barber.

The world changed for Mickey Mantle when the baseball public collectively disdained Maris. Mantle started to be larger-than-life in the popular view. His flaws were largely ignored, his heroics were magnified. He was The Mick to one and all.

Not that Mantle did not give money's worth on his own myth.

In the '61 World Series, against the Cincinnati Reds, Mantle refused the medical wisdom that with the wound on his hip he ought to sit out the Series. He lobbied Houk to let him play, and by the third game the Yankee manager finally relented.

In that game, Mantle chased down a fly ball in the bottom of the first inning, and the exertion opened his wound, leaving blood on his jersey. When he singled in his second at-bat, he ran to first base, in the words of columnist Jim Murray, "like a guy crawling with an arrow in his back."

Such is the stuff of baseball myth, and Mantle continued to provide it through the next three seasons—the last good years for The Mick and the Yankees. In '62 the thirty-year-old Mantle would miss a month of the season when he pulled a groin muscle, tore a muscle in his right thigh, and injured his left knee trying for an infield hit on May 18.

A month later, in Cleveland, a limping Mantle returned to pinch-hit a three-run home run against the Indians' Gary Bell and received a rousing ovation from the Indian fans.

By season's end, playing in 123 games, Mantle would finish with a .321 average, 30 home runs, and 89 RBIs. Then, for the third time in his career, he was voted the American League's Most Valuable Player.

In '63, Mantle, now earning a $100,000 salary, once again came this close to hitting a fair ball out of Yankee Stadium. It happened on May 22, when he hit a pitch by Kansas City's Bill Fischer that struck the facade of the rightfield roof and was rising when it did. A couple feet more and it would have cleared the stadium. As it was, Mantle later called it the hardest shot he had ever hit.

But Mantle's old bugaboo, the injury jinx, struck again that June, in Baltimore. As he leaped to catch a Brooks Robinson drive deep to center, he caught his foot on the chain-link fence there and broke the instep of his left ankle. Mantle was carried from the field on a stretcher. The injury would cause him to miss 61 games.

On August 4, he was back. Before an enthusiastic Yankee Stadium crowd, Mantle stepped up to bat against Baltimore pitcher George Brunet. Mantle drove a curveball into the left-field seats and, so thrilled to have returned with a bang, went out of character by tipping his hat to the joyous crowd.

Because of injuries Mantle would play in only 61 games

THE HARMONICA
BROUHAHA

PHIL LINZ WITHOUT
HIS HARMONICA

In 1964 the Yankees floundered until an incident that August involving the harmonica of a reserve infielder named Phil Linz. It was late August 1964. The Yankees had blown four straight games to their archrival that season, the Chicago White Sox, at Comiskey Park.

The New York team seemed finished, its season shot.

The players and newsmen covering the team trooped onto the bus that would carry them to O'Hare International Airport and then on to the next stop on the schedule. Mantle came aboard, sneaking a couple of beers. Though the team's manager, Yogi Berra, had rules against beer on the bus, well, Yogi wasn't much for making his rules stick.

But while Berra wasn't usually the sort to ramrod his authority, seated up at the front of the bus on this night he was feeling rather testy about the White Sox four-game sweep.

As the bus wended its way through traffic, Phil Linz, a utility infielder, was in the backseat, next to the team's starting first baseman, Joe Pepitone. Linz had in his hand a newly bought harmonica he was teaching himself to play.

The song was "Mary Had a Little Lamb." Linz was playing it by following the numbers on the sheet music that came with the harmonica. He was struggling to get a truly musical sound from the harmonica, his squeaky off-key notes obviously the work of a novice.

From the front of the bus, Berra said something that Linz didn't hear. When he asked what the manager had said, Mantle, ever the practical joker, told him Yogi wanted him to play it louder.

Linz kept playing.

Berra rose from his seat and walked to the back of the bus.

"Hey, Linz. Go stick that harmonica up your ass," Berra said. Linz was taken aback. He rose from his seat and threw the harmonica at Berra, who threw it back at him.

The harmonica hit Pepitone in the knee, whereupon the Yankee first baseman—never one to miss a chance for a laugh—cried out for a medic.

Well, the incident became headline news the next day. The newsmen on board the bus were obliged to write the tale of Linz's atonal harmonica.

That day, Linz walked into Berra's office and apologized. Berra accepted the apology, but told Linz he would be fined $250 since the matter had become public.

When executives at the Hoehner Harmonica company read the story, they contacted Linz and offered him $5,000 to endorse their harmonica.

For Linz, the harmonica brouhaha became profitable.

It also became fodder for clubhouse wits such as Mantle, who needled him: "Phil, I read where you played 'Mary Had a Little Lamb' after we lost all those games in Chicago. It could have been a lot worse. You could have played 'Happy Days Are Here Again.'"

For Berra, his show of anger helped right a sinking ship. As Mantle would say, "In our eyes that was the first time Yogi showed all of us his leadership qualities. It was the turning of the tide. From then on we played great."

The Yankees would go on to win the '64 pennant by one game over the White Sox.

that year, but he would end up batting .314 with 15 home runs and 35 RBIs.

He had become a warrior in spikes, his defiant spirit in combat with his very mortal bones. But that refusal to give in to injuries and his ability to provide high drama each time he returned to action added to the Mantle myth.

But the excellence of the Yankees was no longer guaranteed. The Yankees had been world champions in '61 and '62. But when the Los Angeles Dodgers swept the '63 Series from the Yankees and Houk was replaced as manager by Yogi Berra, the time was fast approaching when the Yankees would never more take winning for granted.

Berra had been with the Yankees for eighteen years as a catcher/outfielder, and '63 had been his final season as a player. The transition from being one of the boys, as Yogi had been, to being boss was not to be an easy one for Berra.

Yogi's way of saying things—called Yogi-isms—had created the image of a somewhat comical bumbler—a naïf, if you will. Though in his time he did utter a malapropism or two, Yogi was no stooge. As Stengel had said, "They say he's funny. Well, he has a lovely wife and family, a beautiful home, money in the bank, and he plays golf with millionaires. What's funny about that?"

As manager of the Yankees, Berra was in the unenviable position of having to command and even discipline players with whom he had clowned through the years. As sportswriter Milton Gross would write: "There was respect for Houk and there was fear of the strong man with the fiery temper. Houk was like the cop on the beat making himself muscular with only his presence while Yogi seemed the kind of guy about whom his player would grin if he displayed a touch of anger."

For Mantle, 1964 would be his last big year, as he batted

.303 with 35 home runs and 111 RBIs. Not bad for a thirty-three-year-old country boy with unreliable legs.

The 1964 season would also be the last time The Mick played in a World Series. Mantle made it special. With the Series tied at a game apiece—Yankees versus St. Louis Cardinals—The Mick broke a 1–1 tie in the bottom of the ninth of the third game when he hit a home run off Cardinal reliever Barney Schultz. It gave the Yankees and pitcher Jim Bouton a 2–1 victory and eased New York ahead in the Series, two games to one.

Mantle would hit two more home runs in the seven-game Series, but it would not be enough to upend St. Louis. The Cardinals' Bob Gibson won games five and seven, and that was that. St. Louis was the world champion.

But for Mantle, with his three home runs against the Cardinals, it gave him a total of 18 World Series home runs, a record that still stands.

The day following the World Series, in a shocking announcement, the Yankees fired Yogi Berra for supposedly lacking a firm hold on his players. Berra was replaced by Johnny Keane, the Cardinal manager who had bested Berra's Yankees in that seven-game Series.

As for Mantle, '64 would prove to be the last season in which the sparks would fly. Time was taking its toll. Looking for a last hurrah, The Mick met old age coming 'round the bend. The result was not pretty.

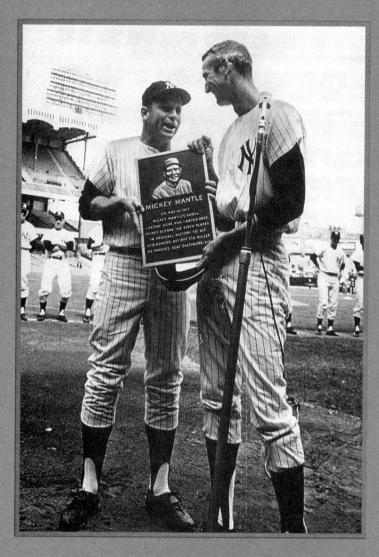

circa 1968

CHAPTER SEVEN

GONE BUT NOT FORGOTTEN

Ａnd so the twilight came.

Mickey Mantle would play another four years for the Yankees, but they would be seasons of struggle, and The Mick would be a dim shadow of the colossus he had been.

The stats are in the neat agate lines of the record book. They go like this: 1965—.255 with 19 home runs and 46 RBIs in 122 games; 1966—.288 with 23 home runs and 56 RBIs in 108 games; 1967—.245 with 22 home runs and 55 RBIs in 144 games; and 1968—.237 with 18 home runs and 54 RBIs in 144 games.

During those four years, the team that had been unequaled for baseball excellence—the winningest franchise in the game's history—became an also-ran, a second-division ball club. Four years of mediocrity. But it was no longer the problem of Del Webb and Dan Topping.

The two men who owned baseball's most prestigious franchise had sold their team to CBS in the midst of the 1964 season. CBS paid $11.2 million for 80 percent of the team, which made the $2.8 million with which Webb and Topping had bought the Yankees nineteen years earlier a very fortuitous investment.

The sale marked another step in the growing commercialization of the game, and accentuated the important linkage of television to sports. In the years ahead, the growth of the major team sports—baseball, football, and basketball—would be measured by the dollars the TV networks doled out. TV would be inextricably tied to the public's awareness of and passion for particular sports, particular players, particular events.

But for CBS, there was little glory in being associated with the Yankee franchise that Webb and Topping dealt them. The team went bad like sour milk. In Keane's first year, 1965, the Yankees plummeted to sixth place—a 77–85 record that marked the first sub-.500 season since 1925. It was not a happy squad. Keane's impersonal style and petty rules only seemed to aggravate the situation. The Yankees were a hard-drinking, party-hearty group, and Keane's insistence on curfews seemed Mickey Mouse to his players. Mantle intensely disliked Keane's drill-sergeant mentality.

Sixth place was unheard-of for the New York Yankees. It would get worse. Twenty games into the '66 season, with the Yankees' record 4–16, Keane was fired, replaced by past manager Houk. But not even Houk could revive the old pinstripe tradition. The Yankees suffered the indignity of finishing dead last in the American League in '66.

Two years later, in what would be his final season, Mantle was a sometime first baseman to spare his beat-up legs. It was harder to spare his feelings, for where once there had been

Signing autographs at the Astrodome.

Berra and Bauer, Rizzuto and Maris alongside him, now there were Jake Gibbs and Horace Clarke, Bill Robinson and Bobby Cox. For New York fans, these were Yankees in name only.

But Mantle was still Mantle. In New York and other American League cities, he got rousing ovations when he stepped into the batter's box. Fans everywhere were paying tribute while they could, but it made The Mick uneasy.

"It's all sentiment," he said. "I'm not sure I like that. They sure as hell aren't cheering me for my batting average."

The sentiment extended to rival players. When Mantle made his last appearance in Detroit, the Tigers had already clinched the pennant. So Detroit pitcher Denny McLain felt there was no reason he couldn't pay his respects to Mantle by grooving a pitch for The Mick in his last at-bat at Tiger Stadium. Word of McLain's generosity was transmitted to Mantle by Detroit catcher Jimmy Price. Mantle got his down-the-middle softy and hit it into the upper deck.

Mantle would turn up at the Yankees' spring training camp in Fort Lauderdale, Florida, in 1969, hoping to play one final year. But his legs were gone and he realized his time had passed. And so on March 1, 1969, well before the season had begun, Mickey Charles Mantle announced his retirement from baseball.

In looking back, he would regret staying on for those last years. For in doing so—in playing when his talent had faded—he had caused his lifetime batting average to drop to .298, a disappointment for a man who thought of himself as a .300 hitter.

But for those who had thrilled to that combination of speed and power (535 home runs, 1,509 RBIs) that Mantle brought to the diamond, he was all the ballplayer a purist could want. For eighteen seasons he had generated excitement when, with a bat in his hand, he would send baseballs flying toward the bleacher seats. In the field he would turn on the afterburners and chase down fly balls that ordinary men simply waved at as they shot by.

He may have had his flaws as a husband and father, but in the world of baseball the standards were restricted to what a man did between the chalked lines. And The Mick had left enough on the playing field to become a hero to a generation. Not to mention his teammates. As Clete Boyer had said after watching Mantle play with that bloody abscess on his hip in the '64 World Series: "Mantle is the kind of man we'd all like to be."

On June 8, 1969, the Yankees honored Mantle by retiring his uniform number 7. In front of a Yankee Stadium crowd of 61,157 and introduced by Mel Allen—a voice from the past— Mantle came out of the dugout and onto the playing field. The crowd cheered and wouldn't stop even when Mantle raised his hands to still the noise.

In back of him stood the men who had made some part of the journey with him—Tom Greenwade, the scout who signed him; Harry Craft and George Selkirk, Mantle's minor-league managers; teammates Joe DiMaggio, Ed Lopat, Gene Woodling, Joe Collins, Phil Rizzuto, Whitey Ford, Jerry Coleman, Gil McDougald, Bobby Richardson, Elston Howard, Tom Tresh, and Joe Pepitone; and even his nemesis in the front office, George Weiss.

DiMaggio presented a plaque to Mantle. Ford gave him a uniform.

Then Mantle spoke:

"When I walked into the stadium eighteen years ago, I guess I felt the same way I feel now. I can't describe it. I just want to say that playing eighteen years in Yankee Stadium for you folks is the best thing that could ever happen to a ballplayer. Now having my number join 3, 4, and 5 kind of tops everything.

"I never knew how a man who was going to die [Lou Gehrig] could say he was the luckiest man in the world. But now I can understand."

Gehrig—dying of paralysis—had spoken to a Yankee Stadium crowd years before, and said he was the luckiest man in the world.

"This," said Mantle, "is a great day for my wife, my four boys [Mickey Jr., David, Billy, and Danny] and my family. I just wish my father could have been here. I'll never forget this. God bless you and thank you very much."

❧ ❧ ❧

"I'm more popular now. . . ."

Dressed in a dark suit and striped tie, Mantle rode around the circumference of the playing field in a golf cart, waving to the fans. Several men and an attractive woman jumped onto the field.

Later, Mantle would tell newsmen: "That last ride around the park—that gave me goose pimples. But I didn't cry. I felt like it. Maybe tonight, when I go to bed, I'll think about it."

For The Mick, the rest of his life lay ahead.

Home was still the ranch house set on the north side of Dallas—the Preston Hollow section. The Mantles had lived there since their move in 1957.

Merlyn's idea that in retirement from baseball Mantle would become a homebody was a pipe dream. Mantle was not cut out for the domestic routine. At home, he would grow restless and bored with the retiree's life—endless rounds of golf at the Preston Trail Golf Club. Being Mickey Mantle, he had ample opportunity to alter the routine. Folks everywhere wanted to get in business with him, or just meet him. So The Mick became the Marco Polo of retired baseball players, opening up trade routes wherever he went. The irony? It turned out Mickey Mantle was

Merlyn Mantle and the boys, from left David, Bill, Danny, and Mickey.

worth more, a whole lot more, as a baseball legend than as the fellow who'd busted his gut on the playing field.

The image of Mickey Mantle took a hit in 1970 when *Ball Four*, a best-selling book by former Yankee teammate Jim Bouton, was published.

Bouton credited Mantle for being a hard competitor and a generous teammate. He showed the boyish side of Mantle, his raucous humor, his readiness for a good time. But in an era when the media were less disposed to pry into the private lives of athletes, the darker side of Mantle, as seen in *Ball Four*, was all the more jarring:

"There were all those times when he'd push little kids aside when they wanted his autograph, and the times when he was snotty to reporters, just about making them crawl and beg for a minute of his time. I've seen him close a bus window on kids trying to get his autograph."

At the time that *Ball Four* was published, there was great consternation among traditionalists, in and out of the press, about what Bouton had revealed. Many of his critics were particularly disturbed by his warts-and-all depiction of Mantle.

But Mantle, inducted with Whitey Ford into the Baseball Hall of Fame in '74, would survive this brush with notoriety. And rather than being damaged by the revelations, his image would somehow grow brighter with time as circumstances conspired to make sports collectibles, and the athletes with which they were associated, increasingly valuable.

For years Topps Chewing Gum of Brooklyn was *the* force behind the most accessible product of what eventually would become a collectibles boom—baseball trading cards. Topps' first set of bubble-gum cards was issued in 1951. And for the next three decades the Topps company had a stranglehold on the baseball card business. That changed on August 15, 1980, when District Court Judge Clarence C. Newcomer ruled that Topps, in conjunction with the Major League Baseball Players' Association, had violated federal antitrust laws. The decision allowed rival manufacturers, such as Donruss and Fleers, to bring out their own sets of baseball cards.

Conventional wisdom at the time was that all those cards would create confusion among collectors and discourage new collectors from coming aboard. Wrong. The sports collectibles

STRICTLY BUSINESS

When early in Mantle's career a con man persuaded him to invest $5,000 in a nonexistent insurance company, it proved to be the first of several disappointing business ventures for Mantle.

But the loss of that money did not deter Mantle from getting into business again and again, sometimes with better results, more often not.

His bowling alley in Dallas was not the grand success that The Mick anticipated. Mantle then became involved with a Holiday Inn in Joplin that bore his name. The Mickey Mantle Holiday Inn proved a better investment; after eight years, the motel was sold and Mantle's share of the deal came to a very profitable $100,000 and an additional $1,000 a month for the next twenty years.

At the time of his retirement, Mantle was involved in launching a restaurant chain called Mickey Mantle's Country Cookin'. As chairman of the board of this publicly traded company, Mantle saw the chain expand to thirteen restaurants before problems developed, and he avoided a brush with the Securities and Exchange Commission as the business went down the tubes.

In 1969 Mantle and New York Jets quarterback Joe Namath became involved with a New York personnel agency called "Mantle Men and Namath Girls," which went belly-up three years later. So did a chain of apparel stores with which he was associated. Real estate investments fizzled; a job in public relations with a life insurance company proved unsatisfying.

When writer Roger Kahn interviewed Mantle for the May 1971 *Esquire*, he found Mantle thinking of marketing an electric batting machine called "Slinging Sam." "Slinging Sam" never did make it to the marketplace, but Mantle kept casting about for a life beyond the playing field. In his retirement, Mantle had a recurring nightmare of appearing at the stadium in his Yankee uniform and trying to crawl through a hole to get to the playing field. While the public-address announcer intoned his name "Nooowww batting, nummmmmber sevvvven"—Mantle would be stuck outside. It didn't take a genius to fathom that The Mick was still torching for baseball. But the baseball-related work offered him—as a coach with the Yankees and as a color commentator on NBC's baseball telecasts—would not work out.

In time Mantle would figure out that the importance of being Mickey Mantle was a business all its own.

business would grow beyond all expectations, generating revenues in the millions and then billions of dollars, enriching merchants and athletes alike even as it corrupted some of them deeply enough to require investigators and courts to set things right.

For a beloved athlete like The Mick, it was tantamount to striking gold—and a far cry from what lending his name out had meant back in the early fifties. Back then, when Topps signed a player to an exclusive contract, he picked out gifts from a catalog as his reward. With a radio or a sports jacket, the bubble-gum company would seal the deal.

But the days of chump change died in the 1980s. Licensing fees from the myriad companies producing trading cards would yield every active major-leaguer an extra $85,000 a season. And as card shows and conventions became increasingly popular, promoters relied on personal appearances of beloved athletes such as Mantle, who would sign autographs for fees that could go as high as $50,000 for a weekend.

That, too, was a radical change from card shows only a decade or so earlier. Michael Aronstein, one of the pioneer dealers in baseball cards, recalled staging a show with three other partners in a union hall in New York's East Village in 1970.

"Afterward," he said, "we put all the money on a table. Singles, and fives, and tens: a big, big pile. Then we began putting aside money for overhead: the rent for the hall, table and chair rentals, flyers, advertising. What was left, we divided. Twelve dollars apiece. We were hysterical laughing."

But by the late 1970s, things were changing. Nearly three decades of 500- and 600-card Topps sets had created a new generation of trading-card aficionados whose objective of assembling complete sets of Topps would lead them to prowl for more esoteric pre–World War II sets and for the rare individual cards—such as the 1909 T-206 Honus Wager, or the 1952 Topps Mickey Mantle. Cards whose scarcity made them valuable. Cards that invariably came with a story.

By 1983, as the boom in sports collectibles was gathering steam, Mantle signed on with the Claridge Casino in Atlantic City.

His job was to fraternize with the casino's high rollers, and, for the golfers among them, play the occasional round on nearby courses. His contract called for him to be available for five days every month, and for that he would receive $100,000, the most he had earned since leaving baseball. It was money he needed for medical expenses. His son Billy was undergoing treatment for Hodgkin's disease. Billy had first been diagnosed with the disease in 1977, when he was nineteen years old. A few months later the disease went into remission, only to recur in 1981.

Once Mantle went to work at the Claridge, the commissioner of baseball, Bowie Kuhn, banned him from all future major-league employment. Kuhn's position was based on Mantle's connection to gambling through the casino. Gambling had been a sticky point for a game that was severely shaken by the 1919 Black Sox scandal, in which eight Chicago White Sox players were accused of taking money to fix the World Series against the Cincinnati Reds. Kuhn saw himself as carrying on the tradition of scrupulous concern that baseball had had for decades about the corruptive influence of gambling. Some approved of what he did in regard to Mantle; others did not. But Kuhn and his ban became irrelevant when he was succeeded as commissioner the following year by Peter Ueberroth, who reinstated Mantle and another baseball great who had taken a similar casino job, Willie Mays.

As the sports nostalgia craze intensified, Mantle discovered that he was the poster boy, if you will, of this phenomenon. Promoters of card shows courted him with lucrative offers, and Mantle began making wads of money—far more than he had earned playing baseball.

When one card show promoter, William Hongach, was indicted in the mid-1990s for tax evasion, he testified that after a show in Atlantic City in 1989, he had paid off certain players in cash, including a box containing $27,000 in U.S. currency that went to Mantle.

While players such as Darryl Strawberry, Pete Rose, and Duke Snider later would have legal problems for not declaring significant income from these card shows, Mantle's attorneys insisted that The Mick had declared *all* his income to the IRS. No problems befell him. Things only got better.

In a 1994 *USA Today* article, reporter Mike Dodd wrote: "Though the [sports memorabilia] market has flattened a bit in the last three years, it's still lucrative. . . . Current players command $7,500–$25,000 for a three- or four-hour appearance. Fees for retired players vary more. . . . New York Yankees legends Mickey Mantle and Joe DiMaggio are at the top of the baseball class. Mantle's fee is $50,000 for 700 autographs, his lawyer, Roy True, says."

Mr. Mint, Alan Rosen, paid him $150,000 for a three-day reunion of the '61 Yankees at Trump Castle in Atlantic City.

It was a strange and totally unanticipated development in Mantle's life. Who could have imagined it? As *Collector's Sportslook* would put it: "But for everything he accomplished during his playing career, it was in retirement that he became an American icon. Twenty-five years after his retirement, he's more popular and, dare we say, more important than he ever was while playing at Yankee Stadium. Why?

"It may be a deep-seated need of mainstream America to

freeze life during a time when things seemed simpler, the 1950s. It may be that people who grew up watching Mantle play are now successful baby boomers with loads of money to spend on memorabilia. . . ."

To those who had grown up in the fifties, baseball surely seemed a more pristine game then. By the eighties and nineties, fans had grown weary of the greed that had overrun the sport, creating lockouts, strikes, and, through free agency, an inflated salary structure that was offensive to the average person. The ranks of the owners and the players appeared to be filled with unattractive egomaniacal sorts who made the national pastime seem a waste of time to a growing number of Americans.

For whatever reason, the public decided Mantle embodied the game as it had been—before Astroturf, exploding score-boards, and domed stadiums. Everywhere he went he was accorded the warmth and affection of a generation nostalgic for what he represented. A simpler time.

Wrote the *Washington Post*'s William Gildea: "Mantle was the centerpiece of a bygone era when teams still rode trains, players carried their own suitcases and sluggers did not stand at home plate admiring their home runs. He ran out his homers quickly with head bent so as not to show up the pitcher."

Mantle's calendar became filled with engagements in which he continued trading on the importance of being Mickey Mantle. Everywhere he went, people wanted some token of Mantle—a signature, a photo, a smile. Others showed up at the fantasy baseball camp Mantle ran with Whitey Ford in Florida. An original painting of Mantle that was used for his 1953 Topps bubble-gum card sold for $110,000 at auction. It was unending, the fascination that folks had for The Mick. As he told *USA Today*: "You know, I dreamed I died, and when I got up to heaven, St. Peter met me at the pearly gates and said I couldn't get in . . .

because I hadn't always been good. 'But before you go,' St. Peter said, 'God has six dozen baseballs He'd like you to sign.'"

❖ ❖ ❖

"I blame myself."

To reporters who had known him as a locker-room lout, the middle-aged version of The Mick seemed new and improved. Mellowed. Open and accessible. And very down-to-earth. "For all his accomplishments," wrote sportswriter Phil Pepe, "Mickey Mantle was a humble man, not filled with himself as are so many superstars. He never considered himself someone special."

The irony was that his own life—never a breeze to begin with—grew messier during this period of rising popular acclaim. Mantle's drinking was intensifying, and the results were not attractive. His behavior embarrassed friends and increasingly troubled Mantle, too, when he heard about it the morning after.

Middle age did not deter him from getting so drunk that he would play his round of golf naked to shock the women on the Preston Trail Golf Club course. Or utter crude and embarrassing remarks in polite company. At that Trump Castle reunion of the '61 Yankees, he was so begrudging a participant that Alan Rosen had to phone his room to get him to appear.

"You know what he told me?" said Rosen. "'Fuck your mother, fuck your show and fuck Donald Trump!' Now, he wasn't being hired to have sex with me in Macy's window for $150,000; all he had to do was show his face. Trump's out there waiting around, so are all his old [Yankee] buddies—and it's in the contract that he has to be there, to take a team picture, all the rest. Was he drunk? Who cares? If he was Steve Howe he'd be in prison, but because he was The Mick it didn't matter what he said or did."

Seen from a distance, his behavior made no sense. Why would someone who was so universally accepted—beloved, even—blur that sweet reality with drink?

The drinking began in the mornings with what Mantle wryly called "the breakfast of champions"—a big glass brimming to the top with a shot or more of brandy over ice, with Kahlúa and cream for good measure, the concoction mixed in a blender.

No matter where he went, the drinking tended to go on through the day and into the wee hours. His increasing consumption was troubling to those who were close to The Mick— his family and old teammates such as Tony Kubek, who remembers spending lots of time with The Mick in New York in the late 1980s, when Mantle was frequently there in connection with his restaurant on Central Park South and Kubek was working for Madison Square Garden Network. Kubek said that other athletes friendly with Mantle tried to steer him off the booze, but Mantle was resistant.

"Unless I had a business engagement," said Mantle, "I'd often keep drinking until I couldn't drink any more. It was when I had no commitments, nothing to do, that I lapsed into these long drinking sessions. It was loneliness and emptiness. I found 'friends' at bars, and filled my emptiness with alcohol. . . . When I was drinking, I thought I was funny—the life of the party. But, as it turned out, nobody could stand to be around me. After one or two drinks, I was real happy. After several, I could be downright nasty."

The drinking had a devastating effect on his family life. It led Mantle to have extramarital affairs, which in turn led to a separation with Merlyn in 1988 and her own drinking

Mantle's hard living off the field left him troubles in his later years.

problem. Mantle's drinking created problems for his sons, whose best chance to know their father came late in The Mick's life as his drinking companions. Mantle likened the feeling to the camaraderie he had felt back in his glory days when he ran wild with Billy Martin and Whitey Ford.

Through the eighties, Mantle believed he had a tolerance

for alcohol that made him invulnerable, his conviction strengthened by those stranger-than-fiction accounts of home runs hit while numbed from a night's debauchery. Upon Mantle's death, *New York Post* sportswriter Peter Coutros would recall the time in the fifties when he found The Mick lying face down on the tile floor of a popular New York nightspot, the Harwyn Club. Shocked by the dead-to-the-world appearance of Mantle, he advised one of the club's owners about the ballplayer's condition. The owner discreetly had Mantle removed with, in Coutros's phrase, "as much dignity as Babe Ruth's body was taken from St. Patrick's Cathedral."

The next morning, the Yankees were scheduled to play a doubleheader against the Washington Senators. Coutros phoned his bookmaker and bet heavily on the Senators, believing that without Mantle it was a sure thing. Wrong. Mantle not only made it into his uniform, he also led the Yankees to a doubleheader sweep by hitting two home runs in each game. Two from each side of the plate.

But the days of wine and roses were behind him by the late eighties. Mantle was experiencing short-term memory loss and blackouts. He developed stomach problems, an ulcer. On airplane flights he began having anxiety attacks. And even though doctors told him his liver was shot and his life was in jeopardy if he continued to drink, Mantle ignored their advice.

Not even the death of Billy Martin on Christmas Day 1989 in a pickup truck crash sobered him up. While there was uncertainty about whether Martin or another man had been driving, authorities said there was no question that Martin would have failed a sobriety test.

Mantle was in denial about his problem. Kubek recalled having a conversation with Mantle not long before The Mick passed away: "I said, 'Mickey, I don't know how many times I've wanted to tell you to stop [drinking].' And he said, 'Tony, it wouldn't have done any good. I wouldn't have listened to you.'"

It wasn't until Merlyn got into a twelve-step program and then his son Danny checked into the Betty Ford Center in September 1993 that Mantle himself began to think seriously about taking care of his drinking problem.

The last straw, he would say, was when he got drunk at a charity golf tournament near Atlanta and that evening referred to the clergyman in charge of the event by saying, "Here's the fucking preacher."

Soon after, he was flying to Palm Springs, California, and, on December 28, 1993, was checking into the Betty Ford Center. It was there he would confront the demons that had driven him to drink. The confrontation would be a painful one.

"It took me a couple of times before I could talk without crying," he said. "I had to talk about how I had screwed up my kids by not being a real father. I said that Mickey, Jr., could have been a major-league baseball player if my dad had been his dad. I've never heard my sons blame me for not being there. But they don't have to. . . . I blame myself."

Mantle, like the others who went through the program, kept a journal. The margins of the journal were filled with words such as *embarrassed, angry, guilty, inadequate, exasperated.*

After leaving the Betty Ford Center, he knew the media would be after him to divulge his experiences with alcoholism. Rather than turn his problem into a cat-and-mouse game with the media, he decided to address it directly. In the April 19, 1994, issue of *Sports Illustrated*, in a cover story written with Jill Lieber one month after his son Billy had died of cancer at age thirty-six, Mantle took readers down the tortuous, alcohol-soaked trail he had traversed. He also did a long televised interview on his alcoholism with Bob Costas.

Then he got on with the life of a recovering alcoholic, which meant limiting his liquid refreshment to Diet Cokes as he made plans to use his experiences as an object lesson for younger people on why they should avoid drinking.

"I think the way he approached it [alcoholism] at the end, and talked about his feet of clay—I think it was another of the attractions he had to people," said Tony Kubek.

Mantle's plans to lend his name, and presence, to antidrug and antidrinking promotions were curtailed by failing health. By the middle of 1995, just months after his mother died in March of complications from Alzheimer's disease, he was constantly suffering from stomach pains that he wanted to believe were merely acid indigestion. By June the pains had grown intense enough for Mantle to be hospitalized at Baylor Medical Center.

His condition was diagnosed as liver cancer.

A Baylor Medical Center physician, Dr. Robert Goldstein, told the media at the time: "There's no doubt that his lifestyle has played a factor in his condition today. I think it's very important for people to take a look at this and and realize what effect lifestyle can have on someone. And hopefully this will get people to reconsider lifestyles."

❧ ❧ ❧

"Don't be like me."

On June 5, doctors said that Mantle needed a liver transplant and categorized him as Priority 1 status on donor lists due to the gravity of his condition.

On June 8, Mantle received a new liver during a seven-and-a-half-hour operation. But when doctors opened Mantle up they found four nodes of cancerous cells in Mantle's bile ducts. The cancer was spreading, and the prognosis was that Mantle did not have long to live.

When the patient emerged from the hospital on June 28, he looked like a shrunken approximation of Mickey Mantle. He had lost forty pounds during the weeks following the transplant.

On July 11, Mantle sat before TV cameras and said, "I would like to say to the kids out there . . . you talk about a role model. *This* is a role model." His thumb was pointing at his chest. "Don't be like me. I mean, God gave me a body and an ability to play baseball. And that's what I wanted to do. Gave me everything. And I just . . . phhhttt." He flicked his hand in a dismissive gesture.

At that time Mantle vowed to increase awareness of the need for organ donors.

On July 13, Mantle underwent a CAT scan. The news was not good. The cancer had reached Mantle's right lung. On July 28, chemotherapy was abandoned.

Also on July 28, Mantle taped a statement in which he revealed the cancer had spread to his lung. The statement was broadcast on August 1, with Mantle saying, "I'd like to thank everyone for all your thoughts and prayers. To all my little teammates out there, please don't do drugs and alcohol. God only gave us one body . . . and keep it healthy. If you want to do something really great, be an organ donor."

At the time of that statement, the doctors who had treated Mantle said that had they known the cancer had spread, they would not have done the transplant.

By August 4, he was back at Baylor Medical Center, receiv-

Mantle's last days, circa 1995

ing blood to treat anemia brought on by the chemotherapy. Soon after, on August 7 and as the cancer spread beyond his lung, he was told by doctors they would not be able to save him.

"When I offered to try to guess how much time he had left, he said he didn't want to know," said Dr. Daniel DeMarco, Mantle's gastroenterologist. "He just wanted to take one day at a time."

Mantle asked to donate his organs so he could help somebody else. But doctors said the cancer was so damaging they couldn't salvage a single organ.

Friends and teammates flew in from all over the country to be with The Mick in his sixteenth-floor suite at the hospital.

Whitey Ford came on August 9, bearing a baseball auto-graphed by the 1995 Yankees with an inscription urging him to get well. The two men joked and talked of old times.

Skowron, Bauer, Blanchard, and Richardson had been in to see him earlier.

Blanchard told newsmen after the four men spent long hours with Mantle: "My heart just sank. I remember this guy carved out of granite. And to see his face withered and shrunk. . . ."

On the way out, Skowron and the others told Mantle they wanted to see him again soon. "I'll let you know when," Mantle said.

In Mantle's final days, Bobby Richardson—often teased by teammates for being a "Goody Two-shoes"—was by his bed-side. Richardson was now a minister and, as he recalled: "We talked about things of a spiritual nature. Mickey talked about his desire over the years to really battle some of the things in his life that proved disastrous over the years. In those last days he had a realization that if he had to do it over again he'd do some things differently."

Mickey Mantle passed away on August 13.

His funeral was held two days later, at the Lovers Lane United Methodist Church in Dallas.

The pallbearers were all teammates: Ford, Skowron, Bauer, Blanchard, Berra, and Bobby Murcer. Richardson gave one of the eulogies. The mourners included Jerry Coleman, Eddie Robinson, Andy Carey, Dr. Bobby Brown, Joe Pepitone, Tom Tresh, Tony Kubek, Stan Musial of the Cardinals, George Steinbrenner (the owner of the Yankees), and Reggie Jackson.

Sportscaster Bob Costas, who even as an adult kept The Mick's baseball card in his wallet, gave another eulogy, say-ing: "In a very different time than today, the first baseball commissioner, Kennesaw Mountain Landis, said every boy

The Yankees pay tribute to Mickey Mantle, 1995.

builds a shrine to some baseball hero, and before that shrine a candle always burns.

"For a huge portion of my generation, Mickey Mantle was that baseball hero. And for reasons that no statistics, no dry recitation of facts can possibly capture, he was the most compelling baseball hero of our lifetime. And he was our symbol of baseball at a time when the game meant something to us that perhaps it no longer does.

"Mickey Mantle had those dual qualities so seldom seen, exuding dynamism and excitement, but at the same time touching your heart—flawed, wounded. We knew there was something poignant about Mickey Mantle before we knew what poignant meant. We didn't just root for him. We felt for him.

"Long before many of us ever cracked a serious book, we knew something about mythology as we watched Mickey Mantle run out a home run through the lengthening shadows of a late Sunday afternoon at Yankee Stadium. . . ."

CHRONOLOGY

1931	October 20: Born in Spanivaw, Oklahoma
1934	Mickey's mother makes him his first baseball uniform
1944	Grandfather Charlie dies of Hodgkin's disease
	Enrolls in commerce High School
1947	Plays second base for the Miami (Okla.) squad in the Ban Johnson League
1949	Spring: Yankee scout Greenwade attends Whiz Kids games at Coffeyville and Baxter Springs
	Offers position on Independence for remainder of season
	Summer: Moves to Independence, Kansas, and begins playing for the Yankee's Class D team
	November: Summoned to appear before the draft board but classified as 4-F due to childhood disease
	December: Begins dating Merlyn Johnson
1950	Spring: Promoted to Joplin Miners, a Class C team in the Western Association
	Hits 26 home runs and 136 runs batted in
	September 17: Promoted to the Yankees as a non-roster player for the last weeks of the 1950 season
1951	February: Arrives in Phoenix for spring training
	Begins training as an outfielder

Signs with Yankees to a major-league contract worth $7,500 for the 1951 season

July 15: Sent down to the Kansas City Blues, a Triple A team and subject to recall

August 23: Recalled by the draft board and once again rejected

August 24: Recalled by the Yankees

Injures knee during the second game of the World Series

December 22: Marries Merlyn Johnson in Picher, Oklahoma

1952: May 6: Father, Mutt Mantle, dies of Hodgkin's disease

May 20: Starts at centerfield

1956 Wins the Triple Crown with a batting average of .353, 130 RBIs, and 52 home runs, and is named the American League's Most Valuable Player

Moves family to Dallas to pursue business venture

1957 Salary rises to $65,000

May 15: The Copa Incident

Dodgers move to San Francisco

Named MVP a second time

1961 Mantle and Maris in home run competition to break Babe Ruth's record

1962 Third MVP award

1964 Plays in his last World Series

1968 Last season with the NY Yankees–.237 average with 18 home runs and 54 RBIs in 144 games

1969 March 1: Announces retirement from baseball

June 8: Yankees honor Mantle by retiring his uniform number 7

1974 Inducted into the Baseball Hall of Fame

1977	Son, Billy, diagnosed with Hodgkin's disease
1988	Separates from Merlyn
1993	December 28: Checks into the Betty Ford Center
1994	March: Son, Billy, dies of Hodgkin's disease
1995	June: Diagnosed with liver cancer
	June 8: Receives liver transplant
	August 13: Dies due to the spread of cancer

Mickey Mantle Baseball Statistics

Year	G	AB	R	H	2B	3B	HR	RBI	AVG
1951	96	341	61	91	11	5	13	65	.267
1952	142	549	94	171	37	7	23	87	.311
1953	127	461	105	136	24	3	21	92	.295
1954	146	543	129	163	17	12	27	102	.300
1955	147	517	121	158	25	11	37	99	.306
1956	150	533	132	188	22	5	52	130	.353
1957	144	474	121	173	28	6	34	94	.365
1958	150	519	127	158	21	1	42	97	.304
1959	144	541	104	154	23	4	31	75	.285
1960	153	527	119	145	17	6	40	94	.275
1961	153	514	132	163	16	6	54	28	.317
1962	123	377	96	121	15	1	30	89	.321
1963	65	172	40	54	8	0	15	35	.314
1964	143	465	92	141	25	2	35	111	.303
1965	122	361	44	92	12	1	19	46	.255
1966	108	333	40	96	12	1	23	56	.288
1967	144	440	63	108	17	0	22	55	.245
1968	144	435	57	103	14	1	18	54	.237
Totals									
18	2401	8102	1677	2415	344	72	536	1509	.298

BIBLIOGRAPHY

BOOKS

Barber, Red, with pictures by Barney Stein. *The Rhubarb Patch*. New York: Simon & Schuster, 1954.

Berger, Phil. *World Series Highlights*. Middletown, Conn.: Weekly Reader Books, 1982.

Bortstein, Larry. *Great Moments of Baseball*. New York: Grossett & Dunlap, 1973.

Bouton, Jim. *Ball Four*. New York: Dell, 1970.

Cannon, Jimmy. *Nobody Asked Me, But . . . : The World of Jimmy Cannon*. New York: Holt, Rinehart, & Winston, 1978.

Falkner, David. *The Last Hero: The Life of Mickey Mantle*. New York: Simon & Schuster, 1995.

Gallagher, Mark. *The Yankee Encyclopedia*. Champaign, Ill.: Sagamore, 1996.

Halberstam, David. *October 1964*. New York: Villard Books, 1994.

Mantle, Merlyn, Mickey, Jr., David, and Dan, with Mickey Hershowitz. *A Hero All His Life: A Memoir by the Mantle Family*. New York: HarperCollins, 1996.

Mantle, Mickey. *The Quality of Courage*. Garden City, N.Y.: Doubleday, 1964.

Mantle, Mickey, as told to Ben Epstein. *The Mickey Mantle Story*. New York: Henry Holt, 1953.

Mantle, Mickey, with Herb Gluck. *The Mick*. New York: Jove Books, 1985.

Mantle, Mickey, and Phil Pepe. *My Favorite Summer:1956*. New York: Island Books, 1991.

Miller, Douglas T., and Marion Nowak. *The Fifties: The Way We Really Were*. Garden City, N. Y.: Doubleday, 1975

Peary, Danny. *We Played the Game: 65 Players Remember Baseball's Greatest Era, 1947–1964*. New York: Hyperion, 1994.

Rosen, Alan, with T. S. O'Connell. *True Mint: Mr. Mint's Price & Investment Guide to True Mint Baseball Cards*. Iola, Wis.: Krause, 1994.

Slocum, Frank. *Baseball Cards of the Fifties: The Complete Topps Cards 1950–1959*. New York: Simon & Schuster, 1994.

Sports Illustrated Presents. *Mantle Remembered*. New York: Warner Books, 1995.

Sugar, Bert Randolph. *The 100 Greatest Athletes of All Time*. New York: Citadel Press, 1995.

——— *The Sports Collectors Bible*. Indianapolis, Ind.: Bobbs-Merrill, 1975.

Thorn, John, and Pete Palmer, eds. *Total Baseball*. New York: Warner Books, 1989 year.

Wolff, Rick, ed. dir. *The Baseball Encyclopedia: The Complete and Official Record of Major League Baseball*. New York: Macmillan, 1969.

PERIODICALS

American Weekly
Baseball Digest
Collector's Sportsbook
Collier's
Current Biography

Esquire

New York Times Sports Magazine

New York Times Sunday Magazine

New York Post

Saturday Evening Post

Sport

Sports Illustrated

Time

USA Today

Washington Post

FILMS

Mickey Mantle: A Magnificent Yankee, MSG Network

Mickey Mantle Day, Classic Sports Network

SOURCES

CHAPTER ONE
REFERENCES

American Weekly; *Esquire*; *Cape* Magazine; *Collier's;* Falkner; Halberstam; Mantle, Merlyn, et al.; Mickey Mantle; Mantle as told to Epstein; Mantle with Gluck; MSG Network; *New York Daily Mirror; New York Daily News; New York Journal-American; New York Times; Sport; Time.*

SOURCES

p. 5 *"Kids nowadays don't"*: *Sport*, December 1964.

p. 5 *"No boy, I think"*: Falkner, p. 23.

p. 6 *"Baseball, that's all"*: *Time*, June 15, 1953.

p. 6 *"It wasn't much"*: *New York Daily Mirror*, October 26, 1952.

p. 6 *"Dad insisted on"*and ensuing: *American Weekly*, July 5, 1953.

p. 8 *"A ground ball, pop"*: *New York Daily Mirror*, October 26, 1952.

p. 9 *"The kids ranged"*: Mantle with Gluck, p. 11.

p. 10 *"When a right-handed"*: *Esquire*, May 1971.

p. 10 *"Dad's book"*: *American Weekly*, July 5, 1953.

p. 11 *"To me this"*: ibid, p. 35.

p. 12 *"And yet the"* and ensuing: Mantle, Merlyn, et al., p. 51.

p. 12 *"It wasn't much"*: *New York Journal-American*, May 9, 1965.

p. 12 *"The very first year"*: ibid.

p. 13 *"We never realized"*: *Sport*, December 1964.

p. 14 *"My folks were"*: Falkner, p. 37.

p. 15 *"The hell you"*: *New York Daily News*, August 14, 1995.

p. 16 *"I drove myself"*: Mantle with Gluck, p. 20.

p. 17 *"I told him"*: *New York Daily Mirror*, October 28, 1952.

p. 18 *"Dad decided Jackie"*: *New York Times*, August 22, 1986.

p. 19 *"I went over to"*: *Collier's*, June 2, 1951.

p. 20 *"I disremember what"*: ibid.

p. 22 *"I don't quite"*: Mantle and Maris, *Cape* Magazine Management Corp., 1961.

p. 22 *"A classic scene"*: Halberstam, p. 81.

p. 23 *"From now on"*: Falkner, p. 59.

CHAPTER TWO

REFERENCES

Collier's; Current Biography; Falkner; Halberstam; Mantle, Merlyn et al.; Mantle with Gluck; *New York Daily News; New York Journal-American;* Thorn and Palmer; *Saturday Evening Post; Sport.*

SOURCES

p. 27 *"Mickey . . . had plenty"*: *New York Journal-American*, May 24, 1958.

p. 28 *"His real weakness"*: ibid.

p. 29 *"Some people are"* and ensuing: *New York Daily News*, August 14, 1995.

p. 32 *"As wonderful and"*: Mantle with Gluck, p. 30.

p. 33 *"But once Mickey"*: Mantle, Merlyn, et al., pp. 40–41.

p. 34 *"We had all"*and ensuing: *Collier's*, July 20, 1956.

p. 34 *"I believe that"*: *Current Biography*, July 1953.

p. 34 *"Tom, you should"*: Halberstam, p. 87.

p. 36 *"We have some"*: *Saturday Evening Post*, April 18, 1953.

p. 40 *"When Mantle was"*: *Collier's*, July 4, 1953.

p. 40 *"You should time"*: ibid.

p. 41 *"All I hear"*: *Saturday Evening Post*, April 18, 1953.

p. 41 *"I had Rizzuto"*: *Collier's*, July 20, 1956.

p. 42 *"That young fellow"*: *Sport*, May 1961.

p. 43 *"I been in"*: *Saturday Evening Post*, April 18, 1953.

p. 44 *"I felt relieved"*: Mantle with Gluck, p. 57.

p. 45 *"You writers have"*: Reported in many sources.

p. 45 *"It's the law"*: *Collier's*, June 2, 1951.

CHAPTER THREE

REFERENCES

American Weekley; *Collier's*; Falkner; Mantle, Merlyn, et al.; Mantle
with Gluck; Miller and Nowak; MSG Network; *New York Daily News*;
New York Journal-American; *New York Times Sunday Magazine*;
Sport; *Time*.

SOURCES

p. 47 *"If the inking"*: *New York Times Sunday Magazine*, June 3, 1951.

p. 47 *"Mantle is the"*: *Sport*, May 1961.

p. 48 *"There it is"*: Mantle with Gluck, p. 61.

p. 48 *"Writers, photographers"*: *American Weekly*,
September 9, 1956.

p. 48 *"The baseball writers"*: ibid.

p. 49 *"With 17 years"*: *Sport*, September 1961.

p. 49 *"I was just"*: *New York Journal-American*, May 25, 1959.

p. 49 *"The kid was"*: *Sport*, September 1961.

p. 50 *"I'm all out"*: *New York Times Sunday Magazine*, June 3, 1951.

p. 50 *"There seems no"*: *Collier's*, June 2, 1951.

p. 51 *"I don't want"*: ibid.

p. 51 *"New York was"*: *American Weekly*, September 9, 1956.

p. 52 *"I never was"*: ibid.

p. 53 *"A small, melancholy"*: *New York Times Sunday Magazine*,
June 3, 1951.

p. 56 *"In the field"*: ibid.

p. 56 *"People up here"*: ibid.

p. 57 *"Put someone in"*: *Time*, June 15, 1953.

p. 57 *"I reacted like"*: *American Weekly*, September 9, 1956.

p. 58 *"I felt like"*: ibid.

p. 60 *"Then he says"*: *Mickey Mantle: A Magnificent Yankee*, MSG
Network

p. 61 *"meeting Holly's"*: Mantle with Gluck, p. 75.

p. 63 *"The Dago's heel"*: *New York Daily News*, August 15, 1995.

p. 64 *"I was afraid"*: *Sport*, September 1961.

p. 65 *"That was the"*: *Saturday Evening Post*, April 18, 1953.

p. 65 *"All that year"*: ibid.

p. 67 *"I knew that"*: Mantle, Merlyn, et al., p. 54.

CHAPTER FOUR

REFERENCES

American Weekly; Cannon; *Collier's*; CMG World Wide; Falkner; Gallagher; Halberstam; Merlyn Mantle, et al.; Mantle with Gluck; Mantle and Pepe; MSG Network; *New York Post*; Peary; *Saturday Evening Post*; *Sport*; *Sports Illustrated* Presents; Wolff.

SOURCES

p. 70 *"Everything had always"*: *Sports Illustrated* Presents, p. 88.

p. 70 *"I was the"*: *Sport*, September 1964.

p. 70 *"Up to Dad's"*: *American Weekly*, July 5, 1953.

p. 71 *"I began to doubt"*: *New York Daily News*, August 14, 1995.

p. 71 *"Back then, I"*: *Sports Illustrated*, Presents, p. 84.

p. 72 *"Casey knew the"*: *Sport*, April 18, 1953.

p. 72 *"We couldn't afford"*: Mantle, Merlyn, et al., p. 57.

p. 73 *"Go chase that"*: Mantle with Gluck, p. 90.

p. 73 *"What did you"*: ibid, p. 91.

p. 74 *"He's the kind"*: Billy Martin Home Page, CMG World Wide

p. 78 *"I hafta keep"*: *Saturday Evening Post*, April 18, 1953.

p. 78 *"He goes out"*: *New York Post*, March 30, 1960.

p. 78 *"Here is where"*: *Collier's*, July 4, 1953.

p. 80 *"The sky may"*: Cannon, p. 46.

p. 81 *"When I came"*: *Sport*, September 1964.

p. 82 *"We were very"*: Peary, p. 208.

p. 82 *"Mickey always said"*: *Mickey Mantle: A Magnicent Yankee*, MSG Network.

p. 83 *"On the way"*: *Sport*, September 1964.

p. 84 *"Mantle isn't the"*: *Saturday Evening Post*, April 18, 1953.

p. 84 *"Mickey could always"*: Falkner, p. 107.

p. 84 *"His anger, his"*: Halberstam, p. 79.

p. 84 *"I ought to"*: *Baseball Digest*, May 1969.

p. 85 *"I offered to"* and ensuing: ibid.

p. 86 *"I got these"*: Halberstam, p. 75.

p. 86 *"Maybe you've got"*: *Mickey Mantle: A Magnicent Yankee*, MSG Network.

p. 88 *"Mickey Mantle wet"*: *New York Post*, November 8, 1996.

p. 89 *"I told the"*: *Sports Illustrated* Presents, p. 89.

p. 91 *"One day on"*: Peary, p. 350.

p. 93 *"Not to take"*: Mantle and Pepe, p. 11.

CHAPTER FIVE

REFERENCES

Barbaer; Berger; *Collier's*; Falkner; Gallagher; Halberstam; Merlyn Mantle et al.; Mantle and Gluck; Mantle and Pepe; *New York Daily Mirror*; *New York Daily News*; *New York Times*; Peary; *Sports Illustrated*; Sugar: *The 100 Greatest Athletes*; Wolff.

SOURCES

p. 95 *"There was verbal"*: Peary, p. 315.

p. 97 *"A tree-mendous ballplayer"*: *New York Times*, April 22, 1956.

p. 98 *"In the 33"* and ensuing: *Sports Illustrated*, June 18, 1956.

p. 98 *"Mantle has more"*: Sugar, *"The 100 . . .,"* p. 263.

p. 98 *"I thought when"*: ibid, p. 263.

p. 98 *"Mickey has grown"*: *Collier's*, July 20, 1956.

p. 98 *"Don't worry about"*: *New York Times*, April 22, 1956.

p. 100 *"Behind the Dodgers"'*: Barber, p. 2.

p. 101 *"Over in River"*: *New York Daily Mirror*, July 8, 1956.

p. 101 *"After being married"*: ibid.

p. 103 *"I didn't want"*: Mantle and Pepe, p. 186.

p. 103 *"Williams conceded the"*: ibid.

p. 104 *"Now I had to"*: ibid.

p. 104 *"I was only the"*: ibid.

p. 104 *"I was standing"*: *New York World-Telegram & Sun*, October 9, 1956.

p. 105 *"I walked away"*: ibid.

p. 106 *"I was nervous"*: ibid.

p. 106 *"And I don't"*: Mantle, Merlyn et al., p. 65.

p. 107 *"How the hell"*: Mantle and Gluck, p. 93.

p. 107 *"If I could run"*: ibid, p. 186.

p. 108 *"It was fantasy"*:Mantle, Merlyn et al., p. 65.

p. 110 *"This guy was"*: Mantle and Pepe, p. 78.

p. 111 *"The bouncer at"*: ibid.

p. 113 *"It's a form,"*: *New York Post*, March 28, 1960.

p. 113 *"Boiled down, consolidated"* and ensuing: ibid.

p. 114 *"It is a"*: *Sport*, August 1960.

p. 114 *"Our life was"*: *New York Daily News*, August 14, 1995.

p. 115 *"All the groundwork"*: *New York Post*, January 21, 1997.

p. 116 *"The Yankees"*: Bouton, p. 38.

p. 118 *"He was sixty-nine"*: Mantle with Gluck, p. 184.

p. 121 *"Make no mistake"*: Gallagher, p. 258.

p. 121 *"He had the"*: Mantle and Pepe, p. 98.

CHAPTER SIX
REFERENCES

Bortsein; Falkner; Gallagher; Mantle with Gluck; MSG Newtwork; *New York Times Sports Magazine*; *Sport*; *Sports Illustrated*.

INTERVIEWS

Bert Randolph Sugar

SOURCES

p. 127 *"All the guys"*: *Mickey Mantle: A Magnificent Yankee*, MSG Network

p. 130 *"Maris was not"*: *New York Times Sports Magazine*, March 31, 1985.

p. 130 *"It had always"* and ensuing: ibid.

p. 130 *"It got to"*: *Sport*, January 1962.

p. 131 *"It felt as though"*: Mantle with Gluck, p. 206.

p. 131 *"When Roger was"*: *Sport*, January 1962.

p. 132 *"After Roger beat"*: *New York Times Sports Magazine*, March 31, 1985.

p. 133 *"Particularly at a"*: Author's interview with Bert Randolph Sugar.

p. 134 *"We'd tell one"*: ibid.

p. 134 *"Like a guy"*: Falkner, p. 153.

p. 137 *"Hey, Linz, go"*: Mantle with Gluck, p. 225.

p. 137 *"Phil, I read"*: *Sports Illustrated*, September 28, 1964.

p. 137 *"In our eyes"*: Mantle with Gluck, p. 225.

p. 138 *"They say he's"*: Gallagher, p. 36.

p. 138 *"There was respect"*: *Sport*, May 1963.

CHAPTER SEVEN

REFERENCES

Bouton; Classic Sports Network; *Collector's Sportslook*; Falkner; Mantle, Merlyn et al.; MSG Network; *New York Daily News*; *New York Post*; *New York Times*; Rosen; Slocum; *USA Today*; Wolff.

INTERVIEWS

Michael Aronstein, Tucker Freeman Smith

SOURCES

p. 144 *"It's all sentiment"*: Mantle, Merlyn et al., p. 83.

p. 145 *"Mantle is the"*: *New York Post*, January 30, 1966.

p. 145 *"When I walked"*: *Mickey Mantle Day*, Classic Sports Network.

p. 145 *"I never knew"*: ibid.

p. 146 *"That last ride"*: *New York Times*, June 9, 1969.

p. 148 *"There were all"*: Bouton, p. 29.

p. 150 *"Afterward, we put"*: Author's interview with Michael Aronstein.

p. 152 *"Though the sports"*: *USA Today*, December 29, 1994.

p. 152 *"But for everything"*: *Collector's Sportslook*, December 1994.

p. 152 *"It may be a"*: ibid.

p. 153 *"Mantle was the"*: *Washington Post*, August 15, 1995.

p. 153 *"You know, I"*: *USA Today*, May 14, 1987.

p. 154 *"For all his"*: *New York Post*, August 14, 1995.

p. 154 *"You know what"*: Falkner, p. 211.

p. 155 *"Unless I had"*: *New York Daily News*, August 14, 1995.

p. 157 *"as much dignity"*: *New York Post*, August 15, 1995.

p. 158 *"I said, 'Mickey"*: *Mickey Mantle: A Magnificent Yankee*, MSG Network.

p. 158 *"Here's the fucking"*: Mantle, Merlyn, et al., p. 28.

p. 158 *"It took me"*: ibid, p. 29.

p. 159 *"I think the"*: *Mickey Mantle: A Magnificent Yankee*, MSG Network.

p. 159 *"There's no doubt*: ibid.

p. 160 *"This is a"*: *Mickey Mantle Day*, Classic Sports Network.

p. 160 *"I would like"*: *Mickey Mantle: A Magnificent Yankee*, MSG Network.

p. 160 *"I'd like to"*: ibid.

p. 161 *"When I offered"*and ensuing: ibid.

p. 162 *"My heart just"*: *New York Times*, August 14, 1995

p. 162 *"I'll let you"*: ibid.

p. 162 *"We talked about"*: *New York Post*, August 15, 1995.

p. 162 *"In a very"*: *Mickey Mantle: A Magnificent Yankee*, MSG Network.

P. 163 *"For a huge portion"*: ibid.

P. 163 *"Mickey Mantle had"*: ibid.

p. 163 *"Long before many"*: ibid.

PHOTOGRAPHY CREDITS

p. iv courtesy of UPI/Corbis-Bettmann
pp. 1, 26 courtesy of UPI/Corbis-Bettmann
p. 2 courtesy of UPI/Corbis-Bettmann
pp. 3, 15 courtesy of Transcendent Algraphics
p. 7 courtesy of AP/ Wide World Photos
p. 21 courtesy of AP/ Wide World Photos
pp. 27, 39 courtesy of AP/ Wide World Photos
p. 33 courtesy of Transcendent Algraphics
p. 37 courtesy of Transcendent Algraphics
p. 46 courtesy of Transcendent Algraphics
pp. 47, 62 courtesy of Photofest
p. 50 courtesy of Transcendent Algraphics
p. 54 courtesy of Transcendent Algraphics
p. 66 courtesy of AP/ Wide World Photos
p. 68 courtesy of Transcendent Algraphics
pp. 69, 81 courtesy of UPI/Corbis-Bettmann
p. 74 courtesy of AP/ Wide World Photos
p. 76 courtesy of AP/ Wide World Photos
p. 94 courtesy of UPI/Corbis-Bettmann
pp. 95, 102 courtesy of AP/ Wide World Photos
p. 99 courtesy of AP/ Wide World Photos
p. 105 courtesy of Photofest
p. 117 courtesy of AP/ Wide World Photos
p. 120 courtesy of Transcendent Algraphics
p. 121 courtesy of Transcendent Algraphics
p. 124 courtesy of AP/ Wide World Photos
pp. 125, 133 courtesy of UPI/Corbis-Bettmann
p. 128 courtesy of Photofest
p. 129 courtesy of Transcendent Algraphics
p. 136 courtesy of Transcendent Algraphics
p. 140 © Ernist Sisto/New York Times Co./Archive Photos
pp. 141,161 courtesy of AP/ Wide World Photos
p. 143 courtesy of AP/ Wide World Photos
p. 147 courtesy of AP/ Wide World Photos
p. 156 courtesy of AP/ Wide World Photos
p. 163 © Reuters/Ray Stubblebline/Archive Photos

INDEX

Stafford, Bill 126
Stallard, Tracy 131
Staub, Rusty 33
Steinbrenner, George 162
Stengel, Casey 34, 40, 41–42,
  43, 44–45, 48, 50, 51, 53,
  57, 58–59, 60, 61, 63, 64,
  69, 70–71, 73, 74, 75, 77,
  78, 80, 86, 88, 90, 95,
  96–97, 111, 118–119,
  120–121, 122, 123, 125, 138
Stobbs, Chuck 79
Strawberry, Darryl 152
Street, Gabby 9, 11
Sturdivant, Tom 40, 96
Sugar, Bert 133
Terry, Ralph 111, 118, 122,
  126
Thomson, Bobby 63
Throneberry, Marv 118
Time 78
Topping, Dan 43, 87–88, 112,
  119, 141–142
Tresh, Tom 145, 162
Trimble, Joe 72, 84
Turley, Bob 90–91, 95, 96,
  118
Ueberroth, Peter 151
USA Today 152, 153
Virdon, Bill 122
Wagner, Honus 151
Washington Post 153
Webb, Del 109, 112, 119,
  141–142
Weiss, George 35–36, 43,
  44–45, 87–88, 89, 109, 111,
  112, 114, 119, 145

Wertz, Vic 102, 103
Wilhelm, Hoyt 119
Williams, Cy 55
Williams, Ted 9, 24, 39, 49,
  90, 98–99, 103, 104, 105,
  107, 109, 111–112
Woodling, Gene 82, 96, 145
Woolard, Alan 13
Wynn, Early 91
Yankee Encylopedia 121
Young, Dick 84–85
Youngman, Harold 108, 114
Zimmer, Don 92

ABOUT THE AUTHOR

Phil Berger is the author of eight nonfiction books and two novels. He has written for *The New York Times*, *The Village Voice*, *Penthouse*, *Look* and *The Washington Post*. He currently writes for the screen and for television.